AN

A TO Z

OF THE NOVELS AND SHORT STORIES

OF

AGATHA CHRISTIE

Ben Morselt

PHOENIX PUBLISHING ASSOCIATES LIMITED

Copyright © Ben Morselt 1985

First published in Great Britain in 1985 by

Phoenix Publishing Associates Limited.

14, Vernon Road, Bushey, Hertfordshire WD2 2JL

ISBN   0 9465 7643 2
ISBN   0 9465 7649 1 (H/C)

Printed in Great Britain by
Billings and Sons, Worcester.

Cover design and illustration by
Denis Gibney Graphics
Chesham, Buckinghamshire.
Typesetting in Beguiat by
Prestige Press (UK) Ltd
Chesham, Buckinghamshire.
Production design by Denis Gibney.

CONTENTS

FOREWORD

A few years ago I mentioned to my friend Roy Tinker, my intention to summarise the novels and short stories of Agatha Christie, for my own entertainment.

Sometime later Gordon Rae of Phoenix Publishing, an acquaintance of Roy Tinker, approached me with a proposal to publish.

Now that the book is completed I would like to thank in particular Martina Fransen and Elsbeth Morselt who helped me complete the task.

For ease of reference we have numbered each of the titles, shown the alternative title and given the year of publication.

Indexes are also provided which list the contents of various short collections and the titles where a 'regular' Agatha Christie character appears.

Also provided is a list of 'whodunnits', where applicable, but obviously you need not use this section if you do not wish to spoil your enjoyment of an unread Agatha Christie mystery.

I hope that readers find our results both helpful and enjoyable.

Ben Morselt

THE MYSTERIOUS AFFAIR AT STYLES

During the first world war Captain Arthur Hastings is invited by John Cavendish to visit Styles Court, a country place in Essex. ·

John's step-mother, Emily has remarried and is living at Styles Court with John and her new husband Alfred Inglethorp. Their guests at Styles Court also include Mary Cavendish and Emily's companions Cynthia Murdoch and Evelyn Howard. During one night of Hastings' stay, on Tuesday July 17th, Emily is found dead. Hastings immediately believes that she has been poisoned and after some reading in the library he is sure that strychnine has been used. After deliberation with John Cavendish, he decides to ask his friend Hercule Poirot for help.

Poirot discovers that the strychnine, used to poison Emily, was dissolved in her medicine, and not in the coffee or cocoa as was assumed.

Alfred Inglethorp, who it seemed disappeared at the time of Emily's death, returns to Styles court. He is the most likely suspect according to Hastings and Miss Howard. Although things look rather bad for Alfred at the inquest, the verdict given reads: 'Wilful Murder against some person or persons unknown!' In the meantime Hastings tries to convince John that Dr. Bauerstein, Emily's doctor, may have committed the murder. John doesn't believe this, since Dr. Bauerstein had no motive, but Hastings is quite sure.

Meanwhile Poirot knows who the murderer is, although he cannot prove it. He invites Inspector Japp and the members of the household to join a little 'reunion' during which he explains who the murderer is and how the murder was committed.

(1)   1920

In the early days of 1915, a secret agreement drawn up in America is dispatched to England by a man called Danvers. Danvers is travelling to England on the Lusitania but the Lusitania is torpedoed by the Germans and sinks.

Danvers entrusts the papers to Jane Finn, an American girl.

Miss Prudence Cowley and Thomas Beresford (called Tuppence and Tommy) are engaged by Mr. A. Carter, who has a very high position in the British Secret Service, as a team of amateur sleuths to save the country by finding Jane Finn.

During their efforts to find Jane Finn they meet Julius P. Hersheimmer, a cousin of Jane Finn. They, Tommy, Tuppence and Julius decide to work together.

They become acquainted with members of Mr. Brown's organisation.

This organisation also tries to secure the secret papers. Tuppence accepts a job as parlourmaid at Mrs. Rita Vandemeyer's where she meets Boris Ivanovitch and Sir James Peel Edgerton, the most celebrated K.C. in England, a friend of Rita Vandemeyer. One day Mrs. Vandemeyer is found dead, poisoned by an overdose of chloral. Tommy goes to Carter in Whitehall and tells him that it is of great importance that the papers are found before the 29th, Labour day.

With the help of Egerton, Tommy and Julius find Jane in a hospital. Then Jane tells her story to Sir James.

(2)   1922

THE MURDER ON THE LINKS

One day Hercule Poirot, sharing rooms with Captain Hastings in London, receives a letter from a Mr. Paul Renauld who is living in Merlinville-sur-Mer.

He tells Poirot he is in danger.

When P. & H. arrive at Villa Genevieve they hear that Paul Renauld has been murdered the same day. It seems that he knew, according to Lucien Bex commissioner of Police, that an attempt was going to be made on his life.

Lucien Bex and Mr. Hautet are charged with handling the case and ask Poirot to assist them in their investigations. According to the story of Madame Eloise Renauld two masked men entered the bedroom and abducted her husband while she was bound by cords.

Francoise Arrichet, the housekeeper tells Poirot that a Madame Daubreuil came to visit Renauld. A letter is found in the pocket of Renauld's overcoat; it is from a woman named Bella.

Mr. Giraud from the Paris Sûretè arrives. He is also in charge of the inquiry. Poirot and Hautet pay a visit to Madame Daubreuil and ask if Renauld did confide anything to her. It seems that a quarrel had taken place between Renauld and his son Jack. Jack loved Marthe Daubreuil but his father would never give his consent for their marriage. Poirot goes to Paris; looking for the murderer of Renauld but meanwhile Jack Renauld is arrested by Giraud. It seems that the letter from a Bella Duveen, found in the coat was destined for Jack and not for his father.

Bella appears. She says she murdered Paul Renauld.

(3)   1923

THE MAN IN THE BROWN SUIT

The action of this novel is reported through the diaries of Anne Beddingfeld and Sir Eustace Pedler. After the death of Charles Beddingfeld, Anne, his daughter, is alone in the world. Returning from an interview for a job, she is a witness to the death of a man in Hyde Park Corner Tube Station.

She also sees another man in a brown suit at that station. With a strange scrap of paper found on the dead body with '17.1 22 Kilmorden Castle' on it, she believes she can solve the mystery.

Mrs. de Castina, a Russian dancer, is found strangled in a room of the Mill House. Anne goes to Scotland Yard but they show no interest. Then she tries to get in touch with Lord Nasby, owner of the Daily Budget. She offers to find out details about the Mill House Mystery and about the Man in the Brown Suit and to write in his paper about them.

Nasby agrees.

She buys a ticket for a boat which leaves on the 17th from Southampton, destination Cape Town. En route to South Africa she meets Sir Eustace Pedler, proprietor of the Mill House at Marlow, the place where the woman was murdered. Is his presence something of a coincidence? She meets Guy Pagett, first secretary of Pedler, and Harry Rayburn, second secretary of Pedler. Also a Mrs. Clarence Blair, a society lady. And Colonel Race, of the Secret Service.

Diamonds are obviously the key to the whole situation. Colonel Race solves the mystery.

(4)   1924

Jimmy McGrath, a Canadian, who lived in Africa, saves the life of Count Stylptitch, Prime Minister of Herzoslovakia. After the death of Stylptitch, Jimmy gets a parcel from Stylptitch containing his memoirs. He is asked to bring those to London on or before October 13th.

Because Jimmy has other plans, Anthony Cade, a friend of his, goes. He also has to give letters from a man called Dutch Pedro to Mrs. Virginia Revel, an English lady at Chimneys. Chimneys is the private country house of the ninth Marquis of Caterham near London.

Anthony comes in contact with Baron Lolopretjzyl, who wants to restore the monarchy in Herzoslovakia. He wishes to buy the memoirs. One day the memoirs are stolen by an Italian, Guiseppi Manelli. Anthony attempts to contact Mrs. Revel concerning the letters. He accompanies her to Chimneys. When they arrive there, they hear the sound of a shot. Count Stanislaus has been murdered.

His real name is Prince Michael Obolovitch of Herzoslovakia. He had an appointment to arrange a loan in the event of his coming to the throne.

Other guests of Lord Caterham at Chimneys are George Lomax, working at Whitehall in the Foreign Office, Bill Eversleigh, assistant of Lomax and two outsiders, Lady Eileen Brent, eldest daughter of Caterham and Mrs. Virginia Revel.

Also at Chimneys is Mademoiselle Brun a governess for Dulcie and Daisy, the Caterham children. Superintendent Battle of Scotland Yard is charged with clearing up the murder. Anthony Cade offers his help for he is suspected too.

(5)   1925

THE MURDER OF ROGER ACKROYD

Dr. James Sheppard is sitting at breakfast with his sister Caroline. He has an early call, concerning a Mrs. Ferrars who has died of a drug overdose. Caroline suspects suicide and though James denies this, he is not satisfied about the case.

It was said that Mrs. Ferrars, a rich woman, would become the wife of Roger Ackroyd, a successful manufacturer, who has already been married twice. It seems strange that Roger Ackroyd's son, Ralph Paton, is in the village, without telling his stepfather, and staying at the local inn. Caroline overhears Ralph, telling his fiancèe and so-called niece Flora Ackroyd how he will be a very rich man if Roger should die. That evening James has dinner at Roger's house. The other guests are Mrs. Ackroyd, Roger's sister-in-law, Flora, Geoffrey Raymond, his secretary and his friend Major Hector Blunt. After dinner Roger tells James in confidence that Mrs. Ferrars had confessed to him that she had poisoned her husband. She had been blackmailed ever since. During this conversation Roger receives a letter which Mrs. Ferrars wrote just before she died, stating the name of the blackmailer. A few hours later, after James has returned home, he receives a call that Roger has been found murdered. The police suspect Parker, the butler, to be the murderer and perhaps the blackmailer, although they find Ralph to be suspicious, too.

Believing in Ralph's innocence, Flora decides to consult the neighbour of the Sheppards, Hercule Poirot. James joins her on her visit and recounts to Poirot the story about the blackmail.

There are some facts in which Poirot takes interest: the door of Roger's room was locked from the outside, the window that was shut earlier in the evening was open and the chair in which Roger was found, has been moved since.

Everything points towards Ralph's guilt: motive, opportunity, means and his being missed, but Poirot believes that these indications are too much and is inclined to suppose Ralph is innocent. Poirot invites Ursula, Caroline, James, Mrs. Ackroyd, Flora, Major Blunt and Geoffrey Raymond for a little conference at his house. He considers them all as suspects but finally points out to them that he knows how the murder was done and by whom.

(6)   1926

THE BIG FOUR

Hastings arrives at the apartment of his friend Hercule Poirot after a stay in Argentina. During their talk Poirot is visited by a very sick man who only murmurs one phrase: 'M. Hercule Poirot, 14 Farraway Street': after repeating this phrase a few times he scribbles down the figure 4 a dozen times, each one bigger than the last. Then he clearly says: 'Li Chang Yen' and tells about the group 'The Big Four'.

After these words he dies. When Inspector Japp is confronted with the dead man he recognizes him as Mayerling, a Secret Service agent.

A visit to the man who knows most about the underground life of China reveals more knowledge about Li Chang Yen.

Mr. Ingles refers them to a man named Whalley, who wrote a letter about how he felt himself threatened by 'The Big Four'. When Hastings and Poirot arrive at Whalley's house, he appears to have been killed.

From the American Secret Service Poirot learns that a British scientist, Mr. Halliday, who was of value to 'The Big Four', has disappeared in France. Hastings and Poirot leave for France where they interview the last persons to have seen Halliday.

Poirot is warned not to interfere but as each member of The Big Four' is revealed, Poirot decides to go after another. One month later they become involved in another murder: that of the globe-trotter Mr. Paynter who has died in his house in England. Written on the paper on his lap were the words 'Yellow Jasmine'.

Poirot finds out that Yellow Jasmine is another name for Gelsemium, a powerful depressant to the central nervous system, which can cause death. A few months later Hastings receives a telegram telling him his wife has been kidnapped. When in contact with the kidnappers, Hastings is forced to write a letter to Poirot in which he is asked to come to a certain house. Thanks to Poirot, Hastings is released. Poirot meanwhile has heard where the headquarters of 'The Big Four' are, in the Dolomites.

Again Poirot and Hastings are captured and brought before 'The Big Four'.

(7)   1927

THE MYSTERY OF THE BLUE TRAIN

Rufus van Aldin, a rich American living in England for the time being, has a daughter Ruth Kettering who has married Derek Kettering; the marriage is an unhappy one. Van Aldin advises her to divorce. He gives her a jewel called 'The Heart of Fire'. Van Aldin makes Kettering an offer of 100,000 pounds to divorce Ruth but he refuses. Ruth is travelling to the French Riveria on the Blue Train. The seat opposite to her is already taken by Katherine Grey. Hercule Poirot is also on the train. Next day Katherine is asked to give information about the lady who was with her in the compartment because the lady has been found dead and her jewel is missing. The maid, Ada Mason is also missing. Mr. Caux and Hercule Poirot are charged with the investigations.

Poirot and M. Carrége have a talk with Ada Mason. She tells them that her mistress changed plans in Paris. Van Aldin asks Poirot to act in this matter. Derek will inherit two million pounds because there is no will.

Derek is suspected. He has a motive and the opportunity.

(8)   1928

14

THE SEVEN DIALS MYSTERY

A group of young people stay at Chimneys, an old castle not far from London. Lady Coote and Sir Oswald Coote, owner of a factory, have rented Chimneys from the Marquis of Caterham. The private secretary of Sir Oswald Coote, Rupert Bateman, nickname Pongo has also joined them. Among the guests is Gerald Wade who sleeps late every morning. They discuss what they can do to get Gerry up earlier. Eight alarm clocks are bought. But the joke fails. Gerald is found dead. Lady Eileen Brent, daughter of Lord Caterham, nickname Bundle, arrives at Chimneys. She finds an unfinished letter in the room in which Gerald died. In that letter is made mention of 'The Seven Dials'.

One day as Bundle is going to London she is involved in the death of a Ronny Devereux. His last words are 'Seven Dials . . . tell . . . Jimmy Thesiger'. Bundle visits Scotland Yard in connection with this case and Superintendent Battle suggests she speaks with Bill Eversleigh. During dinner she asks him about 'The Seven Dials'. He says it is a kind of night club. Next day Bundle returns to 'The Seven Dials Club' on her own and hides herself in a cupboard in the room where the meeting of 'The Seven Dials Club' takes place. Bundle finds out that 'The Seven Dials Club' is a secret group.

(9)   1929

15

THE MURDER AT THE VICARAGE

In the small village of St. Mary Mead live Len Clement, the vicar, his wife Griselda and his nephew Dennis Clement. One day, one of the people of St. Mary Mead, Colonel Protheroe, an unpopular man, is murdered; he is found shot through the back of the head in the study of the vicarage. He has been killed by a pistol belonging to Lawrence Redding, a painter, living in St. Mary Mead.

Inspector Slack and Constable Hurst of the local police are charged with clearing up the case. Miss Jane Marple offers her help. The vicar is also very involved because a lot of people have taken him into their confidence.

Dr. Stone and his secretary are suspected.

Then the vicar receives three summons, which all have to do with the murder. Len pays a visit to the ladies who have written him these letters.

One evening the vicar gets a call from a person who wants 'to confess'. He recognises the voice, goes to meet the caller and finds him lying back in a long chair. Beside him lies a crumpled sheet of paper.

(10)   1930

THE SITTAFORD MYSTERY

Captain Joseph Trevelyan, owner of Sittaford House, has let his house to Mrs. Willett and her daughter Violet.

One evening Mrs. Willet invites round some friends: Mr. Garfield, Mr. Duke, Mr. Rycroft and Major Burnaby. The six of them decide to play table turning. In a message to Major Burnaby the table spells 'T-R-E-V', 'D-E-A-D' and 'M-U-R-D-E-R'! Although no person actually believes in table turning, the message frightens them.

Major Burnaby leaves to pay a visit to Captain Trevelyan but finds him murdered in his house 'Hazelmoor'. He has been struck down by a sandbag.

The doctor supposes that Trevelyan died at approximately twenty past five, the time at which the frightening message was given.

According to Trevelyan's will his estate is divided into four equal portions. One share goes to his sister Jennifer Gardner, the other three to the children of his deceased sister Mary Pearson. Inspector Narracott, in charge of the investigations, pays visits to Trevelyan's relatives.

He finds out that a nephew, James Pearson, saw Trevelyan shortly before his death. Evidence makes it necessary to arrest James.

In the meantime a newspaper reporter Charles Enderby, has got hold of the case. He interviews James Pearson's fiancèe, Emily Trefusis. Pretending they are cousins, Charles and Emily rent rooms from Mrs. Curtis in Sittaford. Emily thinks that during the table turning an accomplice of the murderer betrayed himself and so the six persons who were present then are suspect. Charles and Emily start interviewing them.

Suddenly it becomes clear to Emily who killed Trevelyan. She informs Inspector Narracott about her speculations. Meanwhile the six people who played table turning repeat this experiment. Inspector Narracott enters and arrests one of the persons present.

Remark Alternative title
Murder at Hazelmoor

(11)   1931

PERIL AT END HOUSE

Hercule Poirot and his friend Hastings are spending their holidays in St. Loo, a village on the coast of Cornwall, when they meet a girl with the name of Nick Buckley. She is the last living member of an old family and lives in a mansion called End House, a rather eerie and imposing, tumble-down old place. Poirot, when talking to Nick, hears a little noise but doesn't pay attention to it. A few minutes after he twirls Nick's hat absent-mindedly around his finger and notices a bullet hole in it. The noise must have been a shot, aimed at Nick. She tells them that other 'accidents' have happened to her in the past few weeks. Poirot advises her to ask a distant cousin, called Maggie Buckley, to stay with her.

A few days later Nick organizes a dance, during which Maggie Buckley, wearing Nick's shawl, is found dead. On the evening of the party Nick hears about the death of her secret fiancè, the pilot Michael Seton; the only heir to an enormous sum of money. Poirot finds out that Nick is the only heiress of Michael Seton, which makes her a very rich girl. In the hospital where Nick is staying for her own security, she is poisoned, though not lethally, by cocaine in a chocolate. Poirot decides to pretend she is dead and invites all the suspects to End House and reads to them Nick's refound will.

(12)   1932

In a talk with Hercule Poirot and Hastings, Lady Edgware, also the actress Jane Wilkinson, exclaims that she has to get rid of her husband. She explains that she wants a divorce, which Lord Edgware refuses, to marry the Duke of Merton. Poirot visits Lord Edgware and understands that he is agreeable to a divorce and that he has written so to his wife. This means that either Lord or Lady Edgware is lying.

The following day Poirot learns from Inspector Japp that Lord Edgware has been killed. In an interview Bryan Martin states that he heard Jane Wilkinson utter threats against her husband. Although Inspector Japp first believes she's guilty, she appears to have an alibi, confirmed by fourteen people. Poirot is asked by Geraldine Marsh, Lord Edgware's daughter, to visit her. Poirot also meets Geraldine's cousin, Captain Ronald Marsh, the new Lord Edgware, who thinks it a joke that he is the first person to be suspected. Poirot receives a call from a man named Donald Ross who has something important to tell him in connection with Lord Edgware's death. When Poirot and Hastings hurry to meet him, they find him dead.

Remark   Alternative title
Thirteen at Dinner

(13)   1933

WHY DIDN'T THEY ASK EVANS?

While playing golf, Bobby Jones and Dr. Thomas stumble upon a dying man. The man whispers: 'Why didn't they ask Evans?' and passes away. The only thing the pockets of the man contain is the picture of a beautiful woman. Bobby asks a passer-by, who calls himself Mr. Bassington-ffrench, to stay with the body. The jury's verdict reads death by accident. The victim, recognized as Alex Pritchard by his sister Mrs. Cayman, seems to have fallen down from rocks which caused his death from a broken spine. After reading of the verdict Mr. and Mrs. Cayman pay a visit to Bobby to ask whether Alex said some last words to Bobby. When Bobby's friend Badger Beadon offers him a job as a motor mechanic, unemployed Bobby gladly accepts. That same week he receives a letter from a firm in Buenos Aires, offering him a job at a £1000 salary, which he refuses. Later in the evening, after a game of golf with his friend Lady Frances Derwent, also called Frankie, Bobby is poisoned by something in his drink. Fortunately, the dose of morphine wasn't big enough to kill him. This poisoning and the offer of the job abroad make Bobby and Frankie suspicious and they start their investigations by tracing Mr. Bassington-ffrench. Frankie finds out that Alex Pritchard's real name was Alan Carstairs. Frankie visits her lawyer to find out more about Alan Carstairs. Meanwhile, Bobby goes back to 'The Grange' but is struck on the head and kidnapped. A letter lures Frankie to 'Tudor Cottage', the place where Bobby is held prisoner.

Remark   Alternative title
              The Boomerang Clue

(14)   1934

MURDER ON THE ORIENT EXPRESS

Hercule Poirot is on board the Orient Express. Due to the heavy snowfall, the train stands bound in the Balkans for the night. The next morning one of the passengers, Mr. Ratchett, is found murdered with many stab wounds in his body. Hercule Poirot, is asked by one of the directors of Wagon Lits, Monsieur Bous, to investigate the case. Although the murderer tried to make believe that the killing was done by an outsider, it is certain that he is to be found among the passengers. Poirot starts with interrogating Mr. MacQueen, who is Mr. Ratchett's secretary and who tells him that his employer had received some threatening letters. The interrogation of the other passengers doesn't throw light upon the case. The other passengers are, beside Poirot and MacQueen: Mary Debenham, Colonel Arbuthnot, Mrs. Hubbard, Princess Dragomiroff, Dr. Constantine, Hildegarde Schmidt, Greta Onlsson, Count and Countess Andrenyi, Mr. Hardman, Edward Masterman and the conductor is Pierre Michel. It seems strange that every statement mentions other facts and other suspected persons. Even the wounds don't make clear if the murderer is male or female: some of them are very deep, others are merely scratches. When the murder weapon is found, the doctor states that all wounds were made by that particular knife, which Poirot cannot combine with his suggestion that two murderers are involved. To Poirot it seems as if everybody on the train is lying, so everybody is under suspicion. Poirot invites all the passengers to tell them what really happened.

Remark   Alternative title
Murder in the Calais Coach

(15)   1934

THE ABC MURDERS

One day in June, 1935, Hercule Poirot receives the following letter:

> *Mr. Hercule Poirot, — You fancy yourself, don't you, at solving mysteries that are too difficult for our poor thickhead British police? Let us see, Mr. Clever Poirot, just how clever you can be. Perhaps you'll find this nut too hard to crack.*
>
> > *Yours, etc.,*
> > *ABC*

Two days later Poirot receives a message from Chief Inspector Japp of Scotland Yard that an old woman named Ascher has been found murdered in Andover. Poirot and Hastings leave for Andover immediately: from the police they learn that the time of the murder must be put between 5.30 and 6.5. An ABC railway guide is found on the scene of the murder. An interrogation of Mrs. Ascher's niece doesn't bring them any further. A second letter is sent to Poirot, drawing his attention to Bexhill-on-Sea on the 25th of July. Again, an ABC guide, this time open at Bexhill-on-Sea is found close by the victim.

Scotland Yard and Poirot suppose the murderer is a homicidal maniac, who chooses his victims haphazardly.

On August 30th Poirot receives another letter, announcing a murder at Churston on the same day. When they arrive there, the harm is already done: Sir Carmichael Clarice is found with his head bashed in, with an ABC lying beside him. The murders now get full publicity in the newspapers.

The relatives of the three victims have decided to stand together and ask Poirot for advice. A fourth letter informs Poirot that an accident will take place in Doncaster on September 11th. The group of relatives, Hastings and Poirot arrive in Doncaster. There, another murder is committed. The victim, George Earlsfield, is stabbed and an ABC is left beside him. It seems strange that his initials aren't D.D. Poirot, not satisfied, keeps investigating and invites the group of relatives to tell them how it happened.

(16)   1935

DEATH ON THE CLOUDS

Jane Grey occupies seat no. 16 in an airplane to Croydon from Le Bourget. She has spent her holiday in Le Bourget, where she met the dentist Norman Gale, who is also on the plane. Suddenly the passenger on seat no. 2, Marie Morisot, also called Madame Giselle, is found dead.

Dr. Bryant examines her and discovers a little mark on her. At first it is supposed to be a wasp-sting, but then Hercule Poirot also on board, detects a little thorn with some orange and black silk attached to it. Mr. Clancy, yet another passenger, recognizes it as a South American poisoned thorn.

The blow-pipe from which the thorn is supposed to have been blown is found behind Hercule Poirot's chair. The only persons who could have come near Madame Giselle were the two stewards. But the poisoned thorn was discovered, so the blow-pipe would suggest a murderer sitting in the corridor.

Now Poirot has to find a motive that will lead him to a solution.

Remark   Alternative title
Death in the Air

(17)   1935

THREE ACT TRAGEDY

Sir Charles Cartwright, living in Loomouth, has invited twelve guests for dinner: Mr. Satterthwaite, Sir Bartholomew Strange, Lady Mary and Egg Lytton Gore, Rev. and Mrs. Babbington, Angela Sutcliffe, Mr. and Mrs. Dacres, Anthony Astor, Oliver Manders and Hercule Poirot. During cocktailtime Mr. Babbington takes two sips of his cocktail and dies. Though Sir Charles suspects murder, no traces of poison are found in Babbington's glass.

A few months later Mr. Satterthwaite reads a newspaper which announces Sir Bartholomew Strange's death. During a party in his own house in Yorkshire he died of nicotine poisoning, but his port glass didn't show any traces of nicotine. Mr. Satterthwaite and Sir Charles suppose there is a link between this death and that of Babbington. Satterthwaite and Charles decide to involve Egg Lytton Gore in their investigations, the three of them suppose that Babbington's death is linked with Bartholomew's.

Hercule Poirot joins the three investigators at the request of Satterthwaite. Their list of suspects contains seven persons who were present at Charles' party as well as at Bartholomew's. Each of these suspects is subtly interviewed but the interviews clear them despite the fact that they all seem to have something on their conscience.

Poirot decides to have a sherry party to which, beside Satterthwaite, Charles and Egg, the seven suspects are to be invited. Poirot shows his guests how it is possible to put some (colourless) nicotine in a glass before it is filled.

Later in the evening Poirot receives a telegram from Margaret De Rushbridger, asking him to come immediately because she has some important information on the death of Bartholomew. Poirot finally has the key to the solution of the murders.

Remark   Alternative title
Murder in Three Acts

(18)   1935

CARDS ON THE TABLE

At an exhibition of snuff-boxes Hercule Poirot meets the owner, his friend Mr. Shaitana. In a conversation they have, Mr. Shaitana tells Poirot about his new hobby: the collecting of murderers who have got away with their crimes.

They make an appointment for a dinner, at which Poirot can meet the exhibits. When Poirot arrives at Mr. Shaitana's flat, some guests are already there: the detective-story-writer Mrs. Ariadne Oliver, Colonel Race and Superintendent Battle of Scotland Yard.

Shortly after Poirot's arrival the other guests are announced: Dr. Roberts, Mrs. Lorrimer, Major Despard and Miss Meredith, who are the four murderers Mr. Shaitana mentioned to Poirot as exhibits.

During dinner murder is the main subject, thereafter a game of bridge is suggested in which Mr. Shaitana takes no part. At the end of the game Mr. Shaitana is found murdered. The four 'sleuths' decide to investigate the case. Although they don't have any evidence all four of them have set eyes on a different suspect. Battle, who has an interview with Dr. Roberts, is sure his man committed several murders. Poirot talks with Mrs. Lorrimer.

In a conference between the 'sleuths' they make a list of possible cases of murder that the four suspects are connected with. The investigation of these cases is the next step the 'sleuths' take.

(19)   1936

Miss Amy Leatheran is the nurse of Mrs. Leidner, wife of Dr. Leidner who is the leader of an archaeological expedition in Iraq. Mrs. Leidner suffers from nervous breakdowns, although Father Lavigny, a member of the expedition, simply calls her dangerous and absolutely ruthless. Miss Leatheran and Father Lavigny sense a strange atmosphere at the expedition site. In a conversation between Miss Johnson and Miss Leatheran, Miss Johnson points out that Mrs. Leidner's nervous fears unsettle her husband.

Then Mrs. Leidner reveals the reason for her nervous state. She keeps receiving anonymous letters, announcing that she has to die.

The following day Mrs. Leidner is found murdered by a blow to the front of her head.

Nurse Leatheran informs Captain Maitland, who is in charge of the investigations, about the anonymous letters. It becomes clear that the murderer is a member of the expedition. Because everybody is puzzled about the case, Hercule Poirot is asked to take a look at it.

Finally, after a study of their motives and opportunities, a list of seven suspects is drawn up: Nurse Leatheran, Miss Johnson, Mrs. Mercado, Mr. Mercado, Mr. Reiter, Mr. Emmott and Father Lavigny.

Thanks to a deliberate 'accident' Poirot notices that Mr. Mercado has hypodermic marks on his arm. Then a second murder is committed. Miss Johnson is poisoned by hydrochloric acid, which is used in the archaeological laboratory.

Poirot invites all the members of the expedition to explain to them how it was done and by whom.

(20)   1936

Poirot, on holiday, pays a visit to M. Gaston Blondin, proprietor of 'Chez ma Tante' in London and talks with him about his plans to visit Egypt during the winter. He overhears a young couple making plans to go to Egypt for their honeymoon. Two months later, on his trip on the Nile, Poirot meets the same man, Simon, again but with another woman, Linnet. They have been married. Besides Poirot, Simon, Linnet and Jacqueline, there are a lot of notabilities on the boat, making the same tour: Mrs. Allerton and her son Tim Allerton; Marie Van Schuyler, a rich old lady; Cornelia Robson, cousin of Miss Van Schuyler; Miss Bowers, nurse of Miss Van Schuyler; James Lechdale Fanthorp, lawyer; Mrs. Salome Otterbourne, writer (partly there seeking inspiration for her new book 'Snow on the Desert's Face'); Rosalie Otterbourne, her daughter; Mr. Pennington, American trustee of Linnet; Guido Richetti, archaeologist; Dr. Bessner, a physician; Mr. Ferguson, politician; Louise Bourget, Linnet's maid and Colonel Race.

Poirot has a chat with Linnet. He tells her of his encounter in a restaurant in London with Simon and Jacqueline; they gave the impression of being very happy. Linnet asks him to help her but Poirot refuses. Poirot: 'I will do what I can in the interest of humanity but I will not act for you'.

One night Linnet Doyle is found shot through the head. On the wall of her cabin 'J' has been scrawled in blood, probably by Linnet wishing to indicate her murderess.

Poirot starts the inquiry by interrogating all the passengers.

Salome Otterbourne asks for an interview with Poirot; she says she knows who killed Linnet Doyle.

(21)   1937

DUMB WITNESS

Emily Harriet Laverton Arundell is the mistress of Littlegreeen House, Market Basing, Berkshire. Emily, being unmarried, has made a will, by which her possessions go to the children of her brother, Charles and Theresa, and Bella the daughter of her sister Arabella. On the Friday before Easter in 1936, the 10th April, Miss Wilhelmina Lawson, the companion of Emily, is preparing the house to receive the guests for the Easter-weekend: Charles, Theresa, Bella and Jacob. During the weekend each member of the family shows Emily their greed for her money. In the night Emily falls down the stairs; the blame for the accident is put on Bob, Emily's dog, who left his ball on the top of the stairs but Emily knows better. Lying in bed she writes a letter to her lawyer, Mr. William Purvis, and a letter to Hercule Poirot. In the letter to Purvis she orders a new will, in which she leaves everything to Minnie Lawson. Due to Emily's forgetfulness, Poirot does not receive the letter until the 28th June. When Poirot and Hastings arrive at Littlegreen House, they are told that Emily is deceased, that Minnie has inherited the possessions of Emily and that Minnie now lives in London. Poirot proves that the death of Emily on the 1st of May was murder. The person, who is responsible for the murder, commits suicide.

Remark Alternative title
Poirot Loses a Client

(22)   1937

31

Raymond and Carol Boynton are having a conversation about the necessity of a certain woman's death. Hercule Poirot overhears a part of this conversation and is certain that he will recognise the male voice when he hears it again.

In the same hotel in Jerusalem are Sarah King, Theodore Gerard, an American called Jefferson Cope and, beside Raymond and Carol, the other members of the Boynton family: Mrs. Boynton, whose stepchildren are Raymond and Carol, her stepson Lennox, his wife Nadine and her real daughter Ginevra.

The next day there is an excursion to Petra. The passengers are, beside the aforementioned, Lady Westholme, who is a Member of Parliament and a governess named Miss Amabel Pierce. After a walk, Mrs. Boynton, who suffered from a heart disease, is found dead; a little prick is noticed in her wrist. For her heart trouble Mrs. Boynton used to take a mixture containing digitalis.

Hercule Poirot expresses his suspicions about Raymond Boynton to Colonel Carbury, investigator of the case. He tells him about the words he heard Raymond say in Jerusalem.

The interrogation of the various members of the group throws light upon some new facts. When Carol is confronted, she swears she hasn't done any harm to her stepmother. Miss Pierce tells Poirot that she saw one of the Boynton girls throw a syringe into the stream. This statement, added to the words of Mrs. Boynton that she never forgot anything, makes it all clear to Poirot. He gathers all the members of the party to announce his solution to them.

(23)   1938

HERCULE POIROT'S CHRISTMAS

Old Simeon Lee, a millionaire, invites his whole family to spend Christmas at Gorston Hall. Not all his children are happy with the invitation because of the fact that he treated his late wife very badly. Present are Alfred Lee and his wife Lydia; David Lee and his wife Hilda; George Lee and his wife Magdalene; and Harry Lee. There are two more guests invited: Pilar Estravados, daughter of the late Jennifer Lee who was married to a Spanish artist and who died just over a year ago. Pilar is coming to live at Gorston Hall at the invitation of Simeon Lee. The other guest is Stephen Farr, son of old Ebenezer Farr, Lee's partner in Kimberley, South-Africa. Pilar and Stephen meet each other on the train.

Simeon Lee shows Pilar uncut diamonds in a big safe. On December 24th, Simeon Lee is found dead in a pool of blood. At the moment this happens, all the guests are sitting in the drawing-room, with the exception of David who is in the music-room playing the piano.

Superintendent Sugden of the local police calls Colonel Johnson for help in this case. Hercule Poirot who is staying at Johnson's house, comes with him. Firstly they think that the diamonds have been stolen from the safe but later the diamonds are found. Colonel Johnson assumes it is suicide; Poirot however fancies it is an inside job.

Remark   Alternative title
           Murder for Christmas

(24)   1938

33

MURDER IS EASY

Luke Fitzwilliam has returned to England from the Far East after service as a policeman. In a train he meets an old lady, Miss Lavinia Pinkerton, who tells him she is on her way to Scotland Yard. Luke understands that some murders have been committed in Miss Pinkerton's village; she tells him who is going to be murdered, and makes clear that she knows who the murderer is, without revealing a name. The following day Luke reads in the paper that Miss Pinkerton has been run over by a car. By pretending he is studying witchcraft, Luke enters the village. It seems that there have been several deaths in the village in the last year. By pretending he is interested in burial folklore, Luke learns about them.

The causes of death of the victims are different in each case: Amy Gibbs, a maid, was poisoned by drinking hat paint; Tommy Pierce fell out of a window; Harry Carter, the landlord, fell from a footbridge; Dr. Humbleby died from septicaemia.

Although Luke interviews several villagers and relatives of the victims, he finds out nothing that points to one particular person who could be the murderer.

Remark Alternative title
Easy to Kill

(25)   1939

34

TEN LITTLE NIGGERS

Eight persons are mysteriously invited to go to Nigger Island. By different means of transport they go there, without knowing who their hosts, a 'Mr. and Mrs. Owen', are. On their arrival there appears to be little personnel in the house, only a man-sevant Mr. Rogers and his wife. The names of the guests are: Mr. Wargrave, Vera Claythorne, Philip Lombard, Miss Emily Brent, General Macarthur, Dr. Armstrong, Tony Marston and Mr. Blore. On the first night, after dinner, they suddenly hear a voice, reading a list of various crimes the ten persons present there have committed. After they have compared their invitations, some signed Una Nancy Owen, some Ulick Norman Owen, they come to the conclusion that whoever their host is, he or she has taken a lot of trouble to find out a good deal about them. They start to explain what they are said to be guilty of, making haste to protest their innocence. During these explanations, one of the group takes a drink and slides down from his chair, dead.

The next morning another guest is found dead in her bed. The eight remaining persons decide to leave the island immediately, but the boat which should have taken them away does not appear. Considering the impossibility of someone hiding on the island, they start accusing each other.

Before lunch a third person is killed.

Remark   Alternative titles
And Then There Were None
Ten Little Indians

(26)   1939

Come away, come away, death,
And in sad cypress let me be laid.

Shakespeare

Elinor Carlisle receives an anonymous letter telling her that there is a woman who is trying to make herself popular with Elinor's Aunt Laura, so that she will be remembered in the Aunt's will. Elinor has a talk about it with her cousin Roddy Welman and they conclude that the woman, mentioned in the letter, is Mary Gerrard.

Elinor and Roddy go to Hunterbury, where their aunt lives, to announce their engagement. But, after having returned home, Elinor receives a telegram in which Dr. Lord warns her that Aunt Laura has had a stroke. He asks her to come and she returns to Hunterbury with Roddy.

Aunt Laura dies in their first night there. Since she died intestate, all her property goes to Elinor, her next of kin.

Mary Gerrard dies of poisoning and Elinor is arrested. Dr. Lord asks Hercule Poirot to investigate the case and although Poirot thinks it's rather a difficult case, he accepts.

(27)   1940

ONE, TWO, BUCKLE MY SHOE

Hercule Poirot visits his dentist, Mr. Henry Morley, who lives with his sister Miss Georgina Morley. The patient after him is the banker Alistair Blunt.

In the afternoon of the same day, Poirot receives a call from Chief Inspector Japp that Mr. Morley has shot himself.

From Morley's secretary, Poirot understands that there were three more patients after Mr. Blunt: Miss Sainsbury Seale, Mr. Amberiotis and Miss Kirby. Another person was seen in the house that morning, Frank Carter.

When Japp and Poirot start interviewing the last patients to see Mr. Morley, they find that one of them is dead.

Japp supposes that Mr. Morley shot himself. Poirot is not satisfied with this conclusion and decides to investigate the case.

Poirot has a talk with Mr. Barnes, a retired Home Office employee and patient of Mr. Morley's partner, Mr. Reilly. Mr. Barnes is sure that a group of persons had tried to persuade Mr. Morley to kill one of his patients and when he refused to do so, he was himself shot. Poirot has a talk with Frank Carter and learns that Frank found Mr. Morley dead.

Meanwhile, Miss Sainsbury Seale seems to have disappeared. After finding Miss Sainsbury Seale, Poirot visits Alistair Blunt and tells him the truth.

Remark   Alternative title
The Patriotic Murders

(28)   1940

Tommy and Tuppence Beresford are asked by the Ministry of Requirements to accomplish a job for the government. England is being infiltrated by a group called the 'Fifth Column' who believe in the Nazi aims and are prepared to take over as soon as Hitler has invaded England.

The secret agent who was following them, has been killed. Before he died, he whispered 'N or M Song Susie'. Tommy is asked to replace this agent.

The meaning of the words is known to the Ministry: N is a male, M a female agent, while Song Susie can be explained as 'Sans Souci', a guesthouse on the South coast where N or M must be hiding. Tommy goes to the guesthouse, which lies in Leahampton, as Mr. Meadowes.

The proprietress introduces him to the other guests: Major Bletchley, Mr. Von Deinim, Miss Monton and, to his surprise, Mrs. Blenkensop, who is his own wife Tuppence. In the evening he meets some other guests: Mr. and Mrs. Cayley, Mrs Sprot with her baby Betty and Mrs. O'Rourke.

At first sight the guests all seem what they claim to be. Tuppence pretends she has received a letter from her son with secret information. She puts it in her room and a few hours later she notices that someone has read the letter. Tuppence decides to play this game again, only this time with Tommy on the look-out.

Tommy and Tuppence are convinced that Von Deinim is the traitor. They think that Von Deinim is probably in collaboration with the proprietress of the guesthouse, Mrs. Perenna, and her daughter Sheila.

Then, one day, little Betty Sprot is kidnapped. Every guest starts searching for the girl. She was last seen talking with the foreign woman Carl Von Deinim.

(29)   1941

EVIL UNDER THE SUN

Hercule Poirot is spending his holiday in the Jolly Roger Hotel, Leathercombe Bay, Devon. Among the other guests are the American couple Mr. and Mrs. Odell C. Gardener, Miss Emily Brewster, Miss Rosamund Darnley, Major Barry, Peverend Stephen Lane, Mr. and Mrs. Redfern, the actress Arlena Marshall, her husband Kenneth, his daughter Linda and Horace Blatt.

Arlena seems prepared to start an affair with Patrick Redfern, although Kenneth warns her not to do so. One morning Arlena goes away, not telling anybody, except Poirot. When Miss Brewster and Patrick go for a row they find Arlena at Pixy's Beach, strangled. It appears that the victim was hated and disliked by many people, mostly women and although Poirot is sure that she went to meet someone, he can't guess who. Mrs. Christina Redfern has a motive for having killed Arlena. Kenneth Marshall also had a motive, for he inherits fifty thousand pounds from his late wife and he could have been jealous of his wife having an affair with Patrick Redfern. In an interview with the police Christine Redfern mentions that she knows Arlena Marshall was being blackmailed but Poirot doesn't believe this man killed her, because usually blackmailers don't murder their sources of income. When Poirot and the police inspect Arlena's bedroom, they find several love-letters. In Pixy's Cave, near the place where Arlena was found, a box containing heroin is discovered. Poirot finds out that in the neighbourhood of Whiteridge, where Mr. Lane was vicar, two girls were strangled. This makes him very suspicious. During a gathering of the guests Poirot reveals why the murder was committed.

(30)   1941

THE BODY IN THE LIBRARY

Colonel Arthur and Mrs. Dolly Bantry are awakened in their house 'Gossington Hall' by their maid Mary to be told that there is a body in the library.

Miss Marple, living in the same village, St. Mary Mead, is called immediately. The body is that of a young woman, whom nobody recognizes. The police find her name to be Ruby Keene, dancer in a nearby hotel. It appears that the invalid Mr. Conway Jefferson, a guest in the hotel was rather interested in Ruby Keene.

The police pay a visit to him and meet Mr. Jefferson's relatives: his daughter-in-law Adelaide Jefferson, her son Peter Carmody and Mr. Jefferson's son-in-law Mark Gaskell. It is noticed that his relatives didn't like Mr. Jefferson making a fuss of Ruby and they seem rather happy about her death. Mr. Jefferson informs the police that he had decided to adopt Ruby legally and that he left fifty thousand pounds to be held in trust for Ruby until she was twenty-five.

Miss Marple is asked by Sir Henry Clithering to investigate the case and decides to move temporarily to the hotel where Ruby worked as a dancer.

Then a burnt-up car is found with the charred body of a girl in it. This girl appears to be only recognizable by a shoe and a button of her uniform. The police are inclined to connect the two murders, but are unable to find a motive for either of them.

Miss Marple already knows who the murderer is but refuses to tell Mrs. Bantry as the real murderer is still free but by a clever set-up he walks into a trap.

(31)   1942

41

FIVE LITTLE PIGS

One day in 1942 Hercule Poirot is visited by a girl named Carla Lemarchant. Carla asks Poirot to clear the name of her mother, Caroline Crale, who died in prison after being found guilty of the murder of her husband. First Poirot pays a visit to Caroline's solicitor, Sir Depleach, who is sure she was guilty. He points out to Poirot that there are five persons who had something to do with the case: Crale's best friend Philip Blake, Crale's brother Meredith, Crale's mistress Elsa Greer, the governess Cecilia Williams and Caroline's half-sister Angela Warren, all living at Alderbury.

It seems that just before his death Amyas Crale had decided to divorce Caroline in order to marry Elsa Greer. After his death a bottle containing the poison used was found in Caroline's drawer. She stated that it was in her possession because she had the intention to commit suicide. Poirot starts interrogating the five mentioned persons who he has noted as possible suspects. He asks them to write down an accurate account of the events at Alderbury, sixteen years ago. It is striking that each one of them is certain about Caroline's guilt, except for Angela Warren, who believes Amyas committed suicide.

Hercule Poirot invites the five writers and Carla and her fiancè, John Rattery, to Meredith's laboratory at Handcross Manor, to announce his reconstruction. Carla, introduced to the five persons, can't believe that one of them is the murderer.

Remark　Alternative title
　　　　　Murder in Retrospect

(32)　1943

THE MOVING FINGER

Young Jerry Burton rents, on the advice of his doctor, a house in the little village of Lymstock with his sister Joanna who is to take care of him. On the first day of their stay they receive an anonymous letter, accusing Jerry and Joanna of not being brother and sister.

When Jerry visits the local doctor, Owen Griffith, he learns that he and his sister and Mr. Symmington have received anonymous letters, too, which contain sexual accusations. When Beatrice, the Burton's maid, leaves them because she has received an anonymous letter, Jerry gets very angry. He discovers that anonymous letters have been sent to other villagers as well. One day, one of the villagers, Mrs. Symmington, wife of the local solicitor, commits suicide. Their step-daughter Megan Hunter has become a good friend of Jerry and Joanna, so it's decided that she will stay with them for a few days. It seems obvious that Mrs. Symmington has taken her life because of an anonymous letter she received.

After another letter Jerry decides to contact the police. Some days after Megan has returned home she discovers the body of Agnes Woddell, the maid, in a cupboard. The police assume that Agnes knew who the writer of the anonymous letters was and that is why she was killed.

The vicar's wife, Mrs. Dane Calthrop, invites Miss Marple to investigate, hoping she can throw some light upon the case.

(33)   1943

43

Angus MacWhirter lies in a hospital with a broken shoulder, the result of a failed attempt to commit suicide. Nevile and Kay Strange arrive at Hindhead after a stay in France. Nevile is a famous tennis player who wants to stay in the house 'Gull's Point' for a few months before he starts to travel again. Lady Tressilian who lives at 'Gull's Point' with her distant cousin Mary Aldin has some other guests beside Nevile and Kay: Nevile's ex-wife Audrey Strange and Thomas Royde who is a friend of Lady Tressilian.

For dinner one night Lady Tressilian invites two more guests who are staying in hotels in the neighbourhood: Ted Latimer, a friend of the Stranges and Mr. Treves, a lawyer.

The atmosphere is somewhat tense, with Nevile's two wives being together.

The next day Lady Tressilian receives the message that Mr. Treves has died the night before, returning to his hotel after dinner. He seems to have died of a heart attack. Later the same day, Lady Tressilian is murdered by a blow to the head. Superintendent Battle, who is spending a holiday in the neighbourhood with his nephew Inspector James Leach, is asked by the local police to investigate the case.

They find out that the victim was struck by a left-handed person, and that the murder weapon is a golf club. The butler states that he heard a quarrel between Lady Tressilian and Nevile on the evening of her death.

A closer interrogation of Nevile doesn't relieve him from all suspicion, since he has a strong motive by inheriting a large amount of money from Lady Tressilian. With the help of Angus MacWhirter, the case is solved.

Remark   Alternative title
Come and Be Hanged

(34)   1944

SPARKLING CYANIDE

One night while at her own birthday-party, Rosemary Barton dies after drinking poisoned champagne. It is assumed that she has committed suicide by putting cyanide in her drink.

Although suicide is obvious there are persons who don't consider her death altogether unfortunate. Her sister Iris Marle who inherits all her money; her husband's secretary who believes that George Barton will marry her after Rosemary's death; her friend Anthony Browne who was afraid that she would reveal him as the criminal Tony Merelli; her lover Stephen Farraday who was afraid that she would show his love-letters to his wife; Stephen's wife Sandra, afraid that Rosemary would take Stephen away from her.

George Barton suspecting that his wife has been murdered plans a dinner-party to celebrate Iris, Rosemary's sister's, eighteenth birthday. He organizes it on the same day, 'All Saints' day, and in the same restaurant, 'The Luxembourg' as on the day of Rosemary's death. He invites the same persons that were present then: Anthony, Stephen, Sandra, Colonel Race and Iris.

Colonel Race warns George that this melodramatic dinner could be very dangerous, but George sticks to his plan.

During dinner, George proposes a toast to the memory of Rosemary, drinks from his glass and dies. The guilt of Colonel Race being out of the question, Chief Inspector Kemp considers the five other guests as possible suspects.

Remark   Alternative title
            Remembered Death

(35)   1945

46

DEATH COMES AS THE END

In Thebes, Egypt, in about 2000 B.C., Renisenb is mourning over the death of her young husband. Since he died, she has stayed at her father's house with her child Teti.

Many other people occupy the house besides her father Imhotep, Renisenb and Teti: her brother Yahmose and his wife Satipy, her brother Sobek and his wife Kait, her late mother's companion Henet, her grandmother Esa, her brother Ipy and a man named Hori.

Imhotep is a ka-priest and therefore a very important and rich person. Nofret, Imhoteps concubine, is a source of jealousy. Renisenb is sure that a lot of trouble is caused by Nofret and tells Hori, Imhotep's man of affairs, so. One day, during Imhotep's absence, Nofret has a fight with Kait, about which she informs Imhotep by letter. Imhotep returns a letter, saying that he will turn Yahmose and Sobek out of the house. Yahmose, Satipy, Sobek, Kait and Ipy decide that Nofret has to die.

The next day Nofret is found dead, she has fallen, or has been pushed, from a cliff.

Satipy dies shortly after Nofret, also falling from a cliff.

Renisenb believes that Satipy killed Nofret and committed siucide because she couldn't bear the guilt.

Imhotep is very happy to see that Yahmose and Sobek are much more self-reliant. But when they drink to their health, Sobek's wife appears to have been poisoned and dies. Renisenb is convinced that the poisoning was done by one of the household.

Another death occurs. Ipy is found drowned.

Esa states that she knows who is guilty, although this brings her into a dangerous position.

(36)   1945

THE HOLLOW

The rather vague, but charming Lady Lucy Angkatell invites some relatives and close friends for a week-end at the country house 'The Hollow', owned by Sir Henry Angkatell and herself. The guests are: Midge Hardcastle, who works in a dress shop, Henrietta Savernake, a sculptor, Doctor John Christow and his obedient wife Gerda, anti-capitalist David Angkatell and Edward Angkatell. On the first night they are together, the occupier of the neighbouring house 'Dovecotes', the actress Veronica Cray, drops by to borrow some matches. John and she had an affair fifteen years ago which she wants to start again, but John refuses.

The next day when another neighbour, Hercule Poirot approaches the house with an invitation for lunch, he finds a body with a woman standing over it, revolver in hand.

With his last breath the victim, John Christow, says loudly: 'Henrietta'. At first Gerda, holding the revolver in her hand, is suspected, but she declares that she found John's body and that she picked up the revolver thoughtlessly. Later it is discovered that the bullet in the body did not come from the revolver Gerda was found with.

The revolver with which John Cristow was killed is discovered in Poirot's hedge. The fingerprints on it do not belong to any one connected with the case.

Remark   Alternative title
Murder After Hours

(37)   1946

49

Gordon Cloade, a rich man, marries a very young widow, Rosaleen Underhay. Robert Underhay, her first husband told his friend Major Porter some weeks before that Rosaleen wanted to marry Cloade and that he had agreed to give her a divorce.

Six months later Poirot hears of Cloade's death. Gordon and Rosaleen had lived in Campden Hill with three servants and her brother David Hunter. There had been a blast and three had been killed instantly. Only Rosaleen and her brother survived.

The Cloades are living in Warmsley Heath not far from London. They are: Jeremy, his brother and his wife Frances; Adela Marchmont his sister; Lynn Marchmont, daughter of Lynn; Rowley; Anthony, son of Jeremy; Lionel and his wife Katerine (called Aunt Kathie). Gordon made his last will in 1940, which was revoked by his marriage. Rosaleen gets everything and the family Cloade is in difficulties.

One day a stranger arrives in Warmsley Vale. He is known under the name of Enoch Arden in the Stag where he is staying. Arden says that Robert Underhay is alive and he tries to blackmail Rosaleen.

Enoch Arden is murdered.

Superintendent Spence and Sergeant Graves are placed in charge of the inquiry. Rowley Cloade visits Poirot and asks him to find out who Enoch Arden was. If the dead man is Underhay then Rosaleen was never the legal wife of Gordon Cloade and is not entitled to his money. One day Poirot speaks with a witness in the Stag who says she saw a lady, wearing an orange scarf round her head coming out of Arden's bedroom on the night of his death.

That evening Poirot goes back to the Stag. There is a note from Frances Cloade. She wants to see Poirot.

Remark   Alternative title
There Is a Tide

(38)   1948

CROOKED HOUSE

Charles Hayward meets Sophia Leonides, a granddaughter of Aristide Leonides, a very rich Greek living in England, in Cairo at the end of the second world war. On the day of his arrival back in England, Charles reads in the Times of the death of Aristide Leonides.

Charles wants to see Sophia again and sends a telegram asking her to dinner. At dinner he asks her to marry him but she refuses because of the death of her grandfather. After the death of his first wife Marcia, Aristide remarried a young woman, Brenda. The whole family have been living at Three Gables. In the house are: Brenda Leonides, Roger Leonides and his wife Clemency, Philip Leonides and his wife Magda and their three children Sophia, Eustace and Josephine, Miss Edith de Haviland, sister of the first wife of Aristide, Nannie and Laurence Brown, tutors of Eustace and Josephine. Chief-Inspector Taverner is appointed to investigate Aristide's death as it transpires that he has been poisoned. Charles Hayward also becomes involved because of his interest in Sophia.

Mr. Gaitskill, the solicitor visits the family about the will of Aristide, as it seems that the original will hasn't been signed and attested. Brenda and Laurence are seen as the obvious suspects because of their love affair.

One day, as Charles is going along the passage, he meets Josephine who says 'I should say it is about time for the next murder'.

A further three deaths occur before the case is solved.

(39)   1949

A MURDER IS ANNOUNCED

On Friday, October 29th, the villagers of Chipping Cleghorn read the following paragraph in 'The Gazette': 'A Murder is announced and will take place on Friday, October 29th at Little Paddocks at 6.30 p.m. Friends please accept this, the only invitation'. Naturally the residents of 'Little Paddocks', Miss Letitia Blacklock, her companion Dora Bunner and her two relatives Julia and Patrick Simmons are particularly startled. Letitia expects half the village will visit them around 6.30. The visitors who do come are Philippa Haymes, followed by Colonel and Mrs. Easterbrook, Miss Hinchliffe and Miss Murgatroyd, Mrs. and Edmund Swetterham and Mrs. Harmon.

At 6.30 all the lights go out and a revolver shot is heard twice in the room.

When the lights are on again, a man is found, dead. Nobody knows him, though he is recognized as someone who tried to borrow some money from Miss Blacklock.

The police identify the victim as Rudi Scherz, who has been working in the nearby Royal Spa Hotel at Medenham Wells. All guests at Little Paddocks are interrogated but no real clues come forward so the vicar's wife 'Bunch' Harmon, invites Miss Marple to investigate the case.

When Miss Blacklock's companion Dora Bunner dies, an autopsy shows that she has been poisoned.

Thanks to a coincidence Miss Marple finds out how the lights were fused at 6.30 at 'Little Paddocks'.

Coincidently another villager, Miss Murgatroyd, discovers the same information and tries to tell her housemate, Miss Hinchliffe, but Miss Murgatroyd is later murdered.

Everybody gathers at 'Little Paddocks' where, after an imitation by Miss Marple of a certain voice, the murderer confesses.

(40)   1950

THEY CAME TO BAGHDAD

On the day Victoria Jones has been sacked, she has a talk with a man named Edward who tells her he is leaving for Baghdad the next day.

Having fallen in love with him, Victoria decides to follow him to Baghdad where she manages to get a job as assistant to a Mr. and Mrs. Hamilton Clipp, who are going to see their daughter in Iraq.

In their hotel Victoria meets a girl who looks exactly like herself; this woman, Anna Scheele, appears to be the secretary of an International Bank manager. Having arrived at Baghdad, Victoria realizes that she doesn't know Edward's last name but remembers that he told her the name of his employer, Dr. Rathbone. Unfortunately, Dr. Rathbone informs her that Edward is away for a few days.

Back in the hotel she meets some other British guests: Mr. Dakin, Captain Crosbie, Mrs. Cardew Trench, who work for the British Secret Service. They are worried about one of their guests, Mr. Carmichael, who is missing. At night, suddenly the door of Victoria's room is opened by a man who asks her to hide him. After the police have searched her room without result, Victoria asks the man to come out again, but he appears to be dying. He whispers 'Lucifer-Basrah-Lefarge'. Victoria tells Dakin who has taken care of the body, why and how she has come to Baghdad and Dakin offers her a job. Victoria is sent to Basrah, where she meets Edward, whose last name is Goring and returns with him to Baghdad only to become involved in a series of kidnaps and communist plots.

(41)   1951

To 17525

THEY DO IT WITH MIRRORS

In a conservation between Miss Marple and Mrs. Ruth van Rydock, the latter expresses her worries about her sister, Carrie Louise, who is married to Lewis Serrocold. Miss Marple agrees to go to Stonygates, where Carrie Louise and Lewis live with Miss Juliet Bellever, Carrie Louise's companion, Mildred Strete, Carrie's daughter, Gina, Carrie's granddaughter, Walter Hudd, Gina's husband, Edgar Lawson, the therapist Mr. Baumgarten and the physician Dr. Maverick. Also staying at Stonygates at the moment is Johnnie Restarick's son Stephen who is in love with Gina.

Miss Marple believes that Edgar Lawson, who states he is the son of Winston Churchill, could become dangerous, though Lewis Serrocold and Dr. Maverick don't agree with her.

A telegram announces the arrival of yet another guest, Christian Gulbrandsen, son of Carrie's former husband Eric Gulbrandsen.

Miss Marple overhears a conservation between Christain and Lewis from which she understands that something is the matter with Carrie Louise.

Somebody has put the idea in Edgar Lawson's head, that he really is Lewis Serrocold's son and one evening Edgar shoots at Lewis twice, but misses. In the meantime Mr. Christian Gulbrandsen is found shot dead.

Questioned by the police, Lewis tells that Christian had come to Stonygates to express his belief that Mrs. Serrocold was being slowly poisoned by arsenic.

Lewis asks Miss Marple to act as a watch dog and keep an eye on Carrie Louise.

Ernie, declares to Gina that he knows who the murderer is, but he won't tell her a name. Except for Miss Marple everybody believes he is just boasting. Then one night, he and Alex are found dead.

Although it looks like an accident, Miss Marple is sure that they have been murdered. When she studies the room where Lewis and Edgar had a quarrel at the time of Christian's death, she suddenly realises who the murderer is.

Remark   Alternative title
Murder with Mirrors

(42)   1952

Hercule Poirot is visited by Superintendent Spence, who asks him to investigate the case of Mrs. McGinty's death.

Mrs. Mc.Ginty, who lived in a cottage with a lodger, was murdered while some thirty pounds were taken from her room. The lodger, James Bentley, was tried and condemned to death but Superintendent Spence isn't convinced of James' guilt and has therefore come to Poirot for help. It seems that there are two possibilites if James is innocent. Either the evidence was made up to throw suspicion upon James, or he is just the victim of circumstance. Poirot decides to visit the scene of the murder, a small village called Broadhinny, near Kiichester. He stays in the small guest house there, run by Major and Mrs. Summerhayes, for whom Mrs. McGinty worked as a charwoman.

When Poirot goes through Mrs. McGinty's belongings, he notices a newspaper article about women in old tragedies. It asked where these women were now. The four mentioned are: Eva Kane, Janice Courtland, Lily Gamboll and Vera Blake. Poirot asks himself if Mrs. McGinty has perhaps recognized one of them as a person from her neighbourhood. He visits the writer of the article and discovers that Mrs. McGinty wrote a letter to the newspaper, saying that she knew where there was a photograph of interest.

Poirot visits all Mrs. McGinty's employers: Dr. and Mrs. Rendell, Mr. and Mrs. Wetherby, Mr. and Mrs. Carpenter, Mrs. Laura Upward and her son Robin.

Poirot knows that he is on the right track because someone tries to kill him.

MRS. MCGINTY'S DEAD

When the Carpenters are having a party, to which the Wetherbys, the Upwards, the Rendells, Poirot and Mrs. Oliver are invited, Poirot shows them the photographs from the paper. Mrs. Upward seems to recognize the picture of Lily Gamboll, but doesn't say where she saw it before.

One night, when Robin and Mrs. Oliver are out, Mrs. Upward is strangled.

After the inquest Poirot asks all persons who attended it to come to Long Meadows, his guest house, and tells them who the murderer is.

Remark Alternative title
Blood Will Tell

(43)   1952

After the funeral of Richard Abernathie his family and his lawyer gather in his house. Of his brothers Leo, Timothy and Gordon, and his sisters Geraldine, Cora and Laura, only Timothy, though invalid, and Cora are still alive. Beside Cora the following persons are present at the reading of the will: Mrs. Leo (Helen). Mrs. Timothy (Maude), Laura's son (George Crossfield), Geraldine's daughter (Rosamund), Rosamund's husband (Michael Shane), Gordon's daughter (Susan), Susan's husband (Gregory Banks) and Abernathie's lawyer, Mr Entwhistle.

According to Richards' will the estate is divided into six equal portions: four of these are to go to Timothy, George, Susan and Rosamund. The other two are to be held and the income from them paid to Mrs. Helen Abernathie and Cora Lansquenet. After the reading of the will Cora suddenly says: 'But he was murdered, wasn't he?' When he is notified that Cora has been murdered the day after the funeral, Mr. Entwhistle starts an investigation. Mr. Entwhistle pays visits to all the relatives, but since the interviews with them don't help him, he decides to consult Hercule Poirot. When the whole family, including Miss Gilchvist is gathered again at Enderby Hall, Poirot infiltrates and watches each member of the family closely.

During a discussion about the distributing of some of Richard's furniture, Rosamund points Poirot out as a detective. The feelings of the family on hearing this vary from anger to nervousness. The next morning Helen suddenly remembers something she noticed about Cora on the day of Richard's funeral. She makes a telephone call to Mr.

AFTER THE FUNERAL

Entwhistle to inform him, but is struck on the head
during this call. Poirot assembles the family again,
in the evening, to lay the solution before them.

Remark   Alternative title
Funerals Are Fatal

(44)   1953

A POCKET FULL OF RYE

One day Rex Fortescue is taken ill shortly after his arrival at his office. A doctor is called but some short while later, Fortescue dies and an autopsy shows poisoning by a dose of taxine. Oddly, cereal is found in one of his pockets. There are two sons and a daughter from his first marriage. The daughter Elaine Fortescue lives at Yewtree Lodge as does the elder son Percival Fortescue, partner in the firm, with his wife Jennifer. Lancelot, Rex's younger son, married less than a year ago to the widow of Lord Frederick Anstice, Patricia, lives abroad because of a disagreement with his father.

Rex Fortescue, himself, married not long ago for the second time to a young woman, Adele, made a new will so that his wife Adele and his daughter Elaine would inherit. Also living at Yewtree Lodge are: Miss Ramsbotton, sister-in-law of Rex Fortescue, also called Aunt Effie; Miss Mary Dove, housekeeper; Gladys Martin, parlourmaid and waitress; Ellen Curtis, housemaid; Mr. Crump, the butler. Lancelot and his wife are going to live at Yewtree Lodge.

Not long after her husband's death, Adele is poisoned by cyanide in her tea and Gladys Martin is found strangled with a stocking round her throat and a clothes peg clipped on her nose.

Inspector Neele is in charge and when one day Miss Marple appears at Yewtree Lodge, they decide to work together.

Miss Ramsbotton declares that anybody with Ramsbotton blood in them could be guilty of murder.

Miss Marple concludes that in those murders there is the sequence of an old nursery rhyme like 'the king in the counting-house, the queen in the parlour and the maid hanging out the clothes'.

Lancelot mentions the old Blackbird Mine. A long time ago, Rex Fortescue went to East-Africa with Mr. MacKenzie to investigate the mine. MacKenzie died of fever. Miss Marple and Neele think that the murders are a kind of revenge.

All the rhyme seems to fit together: the blackbirds in the pie, rye in the dead man's pocket, bread and honey in Adele Fortescue's tea.

(45)   1953

Hilary Craven arrives in Casablanca. Her husband has left her and their child has died, so she has decided to commit suicide. Just as she has taken her first sleeping-pill a man who calls himself Mr. Jessop enters her room. He explains that he is a Secret Service agent and tells her about the strange disappearance of many British scientists. The wife of one of these lost scientists, Mrs. Betterton, was a suspect but she died after the crash of an air-plane bound for Morocco.

Since Hilary doesn't care about her life anymore and since she resembles Mrs. Betterton, she is asked to replace her.

Mrs. Betterton's last words were 'Boris', 'dangerous' and 'snow'. This 'Boris' appears to be a distant cousin of Tom Betterton; Major Boris Glydr. Hilary is instructed thoroughly and pretends that she has had a concussion so that it won't look suspicious when her memory fails. There are some other guests at the hotel who get in contact with Hilary: Mrs. Calvin Baker and Miss Hetherington. They find it very interesting that 'Mrs. Betterton' is the only survivor of the crash and talk a lot to her.

Then she is instructed by an enemy agent, M. Laurier, to book a seat to leave Casablanca the following day.

Her fellow-travellers are: Mrs. Baker, Andrew Peters, Torquil Ericsson, Dr. Barron and Miss Needheim. In the middle of nowhere the plane lands and Hilary is told that the other passengers are all famous scientists, while Mrs. Baker is a 'liaison officer'. The plane is blown up to make believe it has crashed with no survivors.

The terminal point of their journey appears to be a remote spot in the High Atlas, where Hilary meets 'her husband', Tom Betterton who doesn't look like the photographs she has seen of him. He doesn't seem surprised that she is not his real wife but whispers to her to play along with him. In confidence Hilary tells Andrew Peters she wants to escape. But then, one evening, Hilary is asked to come to 'The Master', a rich oil magnate.

Mr. Jessop 'cracks' the case.

Remark Alternative title
So Many Steps to Death

(46)   1954

Miss Lemon, Hercule Poirot's secretary, makes a few mistakes in her work and this attracts her employer's attention, because she is never inaccurate. It seems that Miss Lemon is worried about her sister, Mrs. Hubbard, who works in a youth hostel where all kinds of odd things have been disappearing.

Mrs. Hubbard is invited to visit Poirot and it strikes him that, except for a diamond ring and a stethoscope, all the missing things are of lesser value, besides which the diamond ring returned on the same day it disappeared.

Poirot consents to give a lecture at the youth hostel and so meets almost all the tenants: Celia Austin, Nigel Chapman, Patricia Lane, Len Bateson, Valerie Hobhouse, Colin McNabb, Sally Finch, Genevieve Maricaud, René Halle, Jean Tomlinson, Akibombo and Elizabeth Johnston. Four of the foreign students are out: Mr. Chandra Lad, Mr. Gopal Ram, Miss Reinjeer and Mr. Achmed Ali.

Poirot informs them about the real reasons for his visit. Colin, a psychology student, explains to Poirot that he knows that a girl is responsible for the thefts. Celia confesses that she has stolen the missing things and gives Mrs. Hubbard a cheque to replace the stolen goods.

Although the case seems closed after this, Poirot is suddenly notified about Celia's suicide by Mrs. Hubbard who has a feeling there is something wrong about it.

When interviewing the inhabitants of the hostel, Inspector Sharpe, in charge of the case, learns that all of them dislike one or more of their housemates. Sally Finch declares that Celia knew something about someone which was the reason for her being killed. Elizabeth Johnston confirms this statement more or less. During a talk Poirot is having with Valerie, Mrs. Hubbard comes in to tell him that the hostel proprietress, Mrs. Nicoletis has been found dead. Shortly after Patricia is found dead.

After a statement by Mr. Akibombo, all begins to seem clear to Poirot.

Remark   Alternative title
Hickory, Dickory, Death

(47)   1955

Hercule Poirot is called by Mrs. Ariadne Oliver who asks him to come to Nasse House in Nasscombe, Devonshire, immediately.

Poirot arrives at Nasse House, which is owned by the family Stubbs and which has a youth hostel as a neighbour.

Mrs. Oliver, being a famous detective story-writer has been asked by the family Stubbs to organize a Murder Hunt, as part of the village fête. Hercule Poirot is introduced to his hosts: George Stubbs and his much younger wife Hattie, and the other guests: Michael Weyman, architect of a Folly for Sir George Stubbs, Miss Brewis, secretary and housekeeper, a young couple called Alec and Sally Legge, the Mastertons and their bailiff Captain Warburton, and old Mrs. Folliat who lives in the lodge. When Hercule Poirot and Ariadne Oliver are walking the route of the game they find the body of Marlene Ticker, who has been strangled, in the boathouse. Etienne de Sousa, of whose arrival Hattie Stubs was afraid, has arrived at Nasse House at about half past four and is Inspector Bland's first suspect.

Miss Brewis reveals to Poirot that she secretly loves George Stubbs and hates his wife Hattie.

Another murder is committed before Hercule Poirot is certain that Mrs. Folliat knows a lot more than she will tell.

(48)   1956

4.50 FROM PADDINGTON

As Mrs. McGillicuddy is sitting in the 4.50 train from Paddington she sees a woman being strangled in one of the carriages of a passing train. She tells the ticket collector what she has seen, but he doesn't seem to believe her.

In Milchester she gets out and travels on by taxi to St. Mary Mead, where she is going to stay with her friend Miss Marple.

However Miss Marple believes Mrs. McGillicuddy's story and as the newspapers say nothing about the murder she decides to investigate the case by her self. She supposes that the body could have been thrown near a country house, called Rutherford Hall. Miss Marple asks a friend, Lucy Eyelesbarrow to get a post as a domestic help at Rutherford Hall. Lucy succeeds and meets her employers, Mr. Crackenthorpe and his daughter Emma. The other relatives, Harold, Cedric, Alfred, Bryan and Alexander don't live at Rutherford Hall, but do stay there sometimes.

Lucy, when playing golf, finds a powder compact near the place where the body from the train is supposed to have landed. She also discovers a tuft of fur.

Lucy visits a barn and discovers a woman's body in an old sarcophagus and informs Miss Marple and the police. Mr. Crackenthorpe's sons, Cedric, Harold and Alfred, and his son-in-law Bryan Eastly, are present at the inquest and stay on at Rutherford Hall for some days.

There had once been a fourth son, Edmund who just before his death wrote about his intention to marry a French girl named Martine. Recently Martine wrote that she would come to Rutherford Hall with Edmund's son, but she never arrived. If it is true that Edmund had a son, then this boy will inherit the house and it's valuable surroundings.

One night everybody seems to have been taken ill. It is found out that the curry they had for dinner was poisoned with arsenic. Alfred dies. The others, Mr. Crackenthorpe, Harold, Cedric and Emma, recover.

The next day Harold, back in London, is murdered by poisoned tablets.

During a tea party to celebrate Dr. Quimper's birthday, the murderer is recognizd by Mrs. Gillicuddy.

Remark   Alternative title
What Mrs. McGillicuddy Saw

(49)   1957

Arthur Calgary, a geophysicist returning to England after an Antarctic expedition, pays a visit to 'Sunnypoint' where he has a talk with Leo Argyle. Leo's son Jack died in prison after having been found guilty of murdering his mother two years before. Leo's daughter Hester and his secretary Gwenda Vaughan are present, too, when Calgary states that Jack was innocent. Calgary is the only person who can confirm Jack's alibi at the time of Mrs. Argyle's death, but he wasn't able to do so when the trial was on, because he was abroad.

Calgary's statement is rather a shock to the Argylefamily because now the case has to be opened again, with the family coming under suspicion. Calgary learns that at the time of the murder four persons were in or near the house: Leo, Hester, Gwenda and Kirsten Lindstrom, the nurse. Calgary gets angry when he finds that none of the family, not even Jack's wife, cares about Jack's innocence. The family sticks together more than ever, although they know that the murderer is probably among them.

Calgary is visited by Hester who asks him for help.

When Calgary pays another visit to the Argyle family, to finish what he has begun, the truth is finally revealed.

(50)   1958

CAT AMONG THE PIGEONS

In the country of Ramat, where a revolution is about to break out, the Hereditary Sheikh of Ramat, Ali Yusuf, hands a little leather bag with diamonds to his private pilot, Bob Rawlinson, to smuggle them out of the country. Bob decides, without informing her, to hide the diamonds in the luggage of his sister, Joan Sutcliffe, who leaves for England with her daughter, Jennifer.

Six weeks later the wreckage of a plane is found, with two bodies on board, probably those of Bob Rawlinson and Ali Yusuf. Two weeks after this, summer term starts at Meadowbank school. One of the pupils is Princess Shaista, only near relative of Ali Yusuf. Another pupil is Jennifer Sutcliffe. Foreign Affairs decide to send an agent to Meadowbank school, under the name of Adam Goodman, as a gardener.

Jennifer Sutcliffe becomes friends with Julia Upjohn and while playing tennis, notices that there is something wrong with her expensive racquet. Julia and she decide to change racquets.

When the Games Mistress Miss Springer is shot in the Sports Pavilion, all kinds of reasons for her death are brought forward by pupils and teachers but interrogation of the staff and the pupils doesn't throw any light upon the case.

Shortly thereafter a person who calls herself a friend of an aunt gives Jennifer a new racquet and takes away the old one. Then Princess Shaista is kidnapped and that same night another mistress is found killed in the Sports Pavilion.

After a third mistress is killed and all mistresses are gathered, Poirot accuses one of them of having been in Ramat a few months before.

(51)   1959

72

THE PALE HORSE

Father Gorman, a priest in Chelsea, is asked to visit a dying woman, Mrs. Davis, but he arrives too late. A few hours later, Gorman is killed on his way home.

Detective-Inspector Lejeune finds a list of the following names: Ormerod, Sandford, Parkinson, Hesketh-Dubois, Shaw, Harmondsworth, Tuckerton, Corrigan, Delafontaine. The question is: do these names have a connection?

When Mark Easterbrook inherits three water colours from his godmother Lady Hesketh-Dubois, his friend Jim Corrigan tells him that she was on Father Gorman's list.

Mark, Thyrza Grey, Bella Webb and Sybil Stamfordis look for a link between the names on the list and the Pale Horse, an old inn.

Mark thinks that Thyrza Grey, a spiritualist, can cause someone she has never seen, to catch pneumonia and so pays a visit to Mrs. Tuckerton whose daughter Thomasina died recently.

After further enquiries, Mark discovers that a woman visited Father Gorman on the fatal night.

(52)   1961

THE MIRROR CRACK'D FROM SIDE TO SIDE

When Miss Marple is taking a walk, she takes a nasty spill and is invited into the house of Mr. Badcock and his wife Heather. They have a talk about Miss Marple's work and she learns that Gossington Hall, where her friends the Bantrys used to live, has been sold to the famous actress Marina Gregg.

Miss Marple learns that Marina Gregg is married to Jason Rudd, her producer.

During a charity party at Gossington Hall, Mrs. Heather Badcock is taken ill after having a drink and dies while she is having a talk with Marina Gregg. It appears that her drink was poisoned. Since Marina gave her drink to Heather after the latter had spilt hers, the poisoned drink was obviously meant for Marina.

Because Jason Rudd handed them their drinks, he is the first to be suspected.

Chief Inspector Craddock has a talk with Marina Gregg in which she tells him about an anonymous letter she received.

Craddock also finds out that Lola Brewster, an actress who was at the fête, too, was left by her husband Robert Truscott in order to marry Marina. Another suspect is Marina's adopted daughter Margot Bench, who is very bitter after Marina pensioned her and the adopted sons Rod and Angus off.

There are two further killings before Miss Marple, reading old film magazines and hearing that Heather was always a great fan of Marina, finally finds out the truth.

(53)   1962

74

THE CLOCKS

Sheila Webb, typist and stenographer, is sent for a job to 19, Wilbraham Crescent, Crowdean.

Her temporary employer, Miss Pebmarsh, isn't home yet, but Sheila enters, as she was told to do, through the unlatched door. What strikes her first is the enormous number of clocks.

She discovers the body of a man, sprawled on the floor and when blind Miss Pebmarsh enters, Sheila runs out to a passer-by, Mr. Colin Lamb. Detective-Inspector Hardcastle is called and finds out that it was not Miss Pebmarsh who hired Sheila Webb. He also learns that the clocks in her room weren't there when she left the house earlier that day. Hardcastle discovers a printed card on the desk with the name of Mr. R.H. Curry on it of whom Miss Pebmarsh has never heard.

Hardcastle hears from Colin Lamb, who happens to be an Intelligence agent, that he was on a case in the neighbourhood of Wilbraham Crescent.

The neighbours are interviewed without results and so Colin Lamb decides to ask Hercule Poirot, a friend of his father, to throw some light upon the case. In the meantime Hardcastle has an interview with Sheila Webb's aunt, Mrs. Lawton and learns that Sheila was an illegitimate child. Furthermore he understands that her second name Rosemary was painted on one of the clocks, found in Miss Pebmarsh's house. Sheila Webb's colleague, Edna Brent, is startled by the evidence given and has the intention of informing Inspector Hardcastle about it but before being able to do so, she is strangled.

THE CLOCKS

From a girl living in an apartment overlooking Wilbraham Crescent, Inspector Hardcastle learns that a very big laundry basket was brought into Miss Pebmarsh's house on the day of the murder. Colin Lamb, Inspector Hardcastle and Hercule Poirot have a meeting during which Poirot states that he knows who the murderer is.

(54)   1963

A CARIBBEAN MYSTERY

Miss Marple has received as a present from her nephew Raymond West a journey to the Caribbean Island St. Hororé. She is staying in the Golden Palm Hotel, which is run by Tim and Molly Kendal. One of the important guests of the hotel is Mr. Rafiel, a very rich man, who is crippled and therefore has a male nurse-attendant, Arthur Jackson.

Another guest is Major Polgrave, who tells Miss Marple the story of a man who has twice married and afterwards murdered his wife for her money. The same evening the Major dies from an overdose.

Miss Marple suspects that the Major has been murdered. Some time later one of the room-maids, who had her suspicions about the origin of the bottle in Major Polgrave's room, is murdered. Miss Marple is still in the dark until another murder is committed; thereupon Miss Marple knows who the killer is.

(55)   1964

AT BERTRAM'S HOTEL

Miss Marple is spending some time at the old-fashioned, Bertram's Hotel as a treat from her relatives Joan and Raymond West. During Miss Marple's stay some of the other guests are: Colonel Luscombe and his pupil Elvira Blake and the woman who is, unknown to Elvira, her mother, Lady Bess Sedgewick.

In the meantime a conference is held at Scotland Yard about the increasing amount of big scale robberies. It is supposed that there is one planner, one mastermind behind all those crimes. One person in particular, Chief-Inspector Fred Davy, also called 'Father', is in charge of the investigations.

When one of the guests, the absent-minded Canon Pennyfather, is missing, people are not worried at first, because he has 'disappeared' before, due to his absent-mindedness. Then Scotland Yard is informed and Chief-Inspector Davy pays a visit to Bertram's Hotel to interrogate some of the guests.

A few days later Canon Pennyfather turns up again. He has concussion and he can't remember how he got to Milton St. where he was found. Meanwhile, Chief-Inspector Davy is quite sure that Bertram's Hotel has got something to do with the organised robberies.

Miss Marple has the feeling that something evil is going to happen, perhaps murder. Although Chief-Inspector Davy doesn't believe her she turns out to be right. One night, the commissionaire Michael Gorman is shot. It appears that he ran forward when Elvira was being shot at. Elvira states that there has been an attack on her life once before.

A talk with Elvira's lawyer and trustee reveals to Davy the fact that she is the heiress of a large amount of money, left to her by her father. Ladislaus Malinkowski is questioned because it was his pistol the shots were fired with. Miss Marple is sure that Canon Pennyfather has what is called in German a 'doppelganger'.

Chief Inspector Davy discovers how the robberies are organized.

(56)   1965

THIRD GIRL

One morning Hercule Poirot is visited by a young woman who has told George, Poirot's butler, that she has perhaps committed a murder.

When Poirot visits his friend, the writer of detective stories Mrs. Ariadne Oliver, the fact is brought out that the girl is known to Mrs. Oliver as Norma Restarick.

Mrs. Oliver goes to Norma's apartment in Borodene Mansions, but her roommates, Claudia Reece-Holland and Frances Cary, declare that they don't know where Norma is.

Poirot calls at 'Crosshedges', the country house of Norma's parents, where he meets Mary Restarick, Norma's step-mother, an artist called David Baker and Sir Roderick Horsefield, Norma's great-uncle. Norma doesn't seem to be there, either. An interview with the door-keeper at Borodene Mansions reveals the fact that Norma was once found with a revolver in her hand, after a shot was heard. Apparently nothing had happened, although Norma stated that she had seen blood and that there was some blood lying on the ground.

Mrs. Oliver decides to visit Borodene Mansions again and hears that an elderly lady named Louise Charpentier has fallen from a balcony on the seventh floor. Her apartment number (76) is the reverse from Norma's.

Later she discovers Norma and David and overhears the conversation between them, during which Norma declares that she has found a half-empty bottle of poison in a drawer in her room at 'Crosshedges'.

Shortly afterwards, Norma tries to commit suicide but is saved by a doctor named Stillingfleet who takes her secretly to a private hospital. Poirot is engaged by Norma's father, Andrew, to trace her, and pays another visit to Borodene Mansions where he finds the body of David Baker with Norma standing beside it, knife in hand.

During a subsequent gathering, Hercule Poirot reveals the truth.

(57)   1966

ENDLESS NIGHT

Some are born to Sweet Delight
Some are born to Endless Night.
William Blake.

Michael Rogers, is walking idly about in the village of Kingston Bishop when he notices the announcement of the auction of the property 'The Towers'. When talking to a local, he hears that 'The Towers' is also called 'Gipsy's Acre' because all kinds of accidents take place there; a gipsy curse is said to be laying not only on the house, but on the land as well.

In the same village Michael meets and falls in love with a girl, Fenella (Ellie) Goodman. Ellie reveals to Michael that her real name is Guteman and that she is one of the richest women in America and therefore able to buy 'Gipsy's Acre' for Michael and herself. The architect Rudolf Santonix, a friend of Michael's is asked to design a house for them on the land of 'Gipsy's Acre'.

Ellie is warned by a gipsy from the neighbourhood not to live at 'Gipsy's Acre', which frightens her. During the building of the house some small accidents happen.

Because Ellie is restless and doesn't feel well, Greta, Ellie's companion, comes to live with them although Michael points out clearly to Ellie that he hates Greta. When Michael is at an auction with Major Phillpot, Ellie falls from her horse and dies. It is suggested that the gipsy Mrs. Lee frightened the horse so that it threw Ellie but Mrs. Lee can't be found anywhere.

Greta stays at 'Gipsy's Acre' after Ellie's death and during the funeral in America, Michael receives the message that Mrs. Lee has been found dead.

(58)   1967

BY THE PRICKING OF MY THUMBS

Mr. Thomas and Mrs. Prudence Beresford, Tommy and Tuppence, are visiting Tommy's aunt Ada Fanshawe, who is living in Sunny Ridge, a home for elderly ladies. During this visit Tuppence meets Mrs. Lancaster, who starts the conversation with the question 'Is it your poor child?'

When Aunt Ada dies, Tommy and Tuppence visit Sunny Ridge again and hear that Mrs. Lancaster has left the home and been taken away by a relative, Mrs. Johnson.

She has left a picture, the picture shows a house at a canal, a house that Tuppence has seen before.

Tuppence tries to write to Mrs. Lancaster, but there is no way to reach her. Her next activity is to find the house and she succeeds: the house is near Sutton Chancellor. Trying to find out more about Mrs. Lancaster, Tuppence hears about child murders that took place some years ago. The murderer or murderess was never found, although some of the inhabitants were suspected, among them Sir Philip Starke.

Tommy is informed that a Mr. Eccles, who acts as an intermediate to Mrs. Johnson, is involved in criminal activities. The house at the canal could have been the headquarters of the gang Eccles is connected with.

By further hunting Tommy and Tuppence uncover amazing facts about Mrs. Lancaster.

Tuppence finds out who was responsible for the death of the children in Sutton Chancellor.

(59)   1968

84

HALLOWE'EN PARTY

Mrs. Ariadne Oliver, the detective novelist and a friend of Hercule Poirot, is visiting her friend Judith Butler in Woodleigh Common. Judith is a widow and has one daughter, Miranda. Ariadne is introduced to Mrs. Rowena Drake, in whose house preparations are being made for the Hallowe'en party that night. During these preparations one of the guests, Joyce Reynolds, tells of a murder she saw once years ago, but that at the time didn't know it was a murder.

During the evening-party Joyce is murdered.

Ariadne calls Poirot for help and he starts, with the help of his retired friend Superintendent Spence, to investigate past murders and suspicious natural deaths. He is hampered by the circumstances, that everybody is convinced that Joyce was a liar.

One of the cases that attracts his interest is the death of Mrs. Louise Llewellyn-Smythe; Louise had an au-pair girl, Olga Seminoff, to whom she left all her money, although in earlier wills she left it to her niece Rowena Drake. Poirot finds out that it is possible that Louise changed her will, because she discovered that Rowena had an affair.

When Leopold Reynolds, a younger brother of Joyce, is drowned, Poirot suspects that Leopold blackmailed the murderer.

By sending Judith and Miranda to the home of Ariadne he tries to prevent the murder of Miranda as she has the answer to the case.

(60)   1969

At Frankfurt Airport Sir Stafford Nye, a diplomat with a disappointing career, is asked by a girl who resembles his late sister Pamela, if he will allow her to impersonate him, while he has to pretend to have been drugged and robbed.

Stafford Nye agrees but back in London, he is nearly hit by a car.

He reads a paragraph in the paper: 'Passenger from Frankfurt, Thursday Nov. 11, Hungerford Bridge 7.20' and decides to go there at the mentioned time. He receives a ticket for the opera 'Siegfried' and finds that the seat next to his is occupied by Daphne Theodofanous, the girl at the airport. She passes him a programme with, what sems to him some musical notations on it, and speaks the words 'The young Siegfried'.

Stafford Nye learns about an evil Youth Movement and that the term 'The young Siegfried' has got something to do with it. At dinner at the American Embassy Stafford Nye meets the girl from the airport again: she introduces herself as Countess Renata Zerkowski, which appears to be her real name. She takes him to her house, where he meets the very rich Mr. Robinson, Sir James Kleek, Lord Altamount and Mr. Horsham. They tell him they have formed a group to dismantle this Youth Movement.

The centre of the movement seems to be sited in Germany, so it's decided that Stafford Nye and Renata will go there. In confidence Renata tells him that she supposes one of their group to be a traitor.

According to British investigators 'Big Charlotte' is the financial force behind it all.

Thanks to Sir Stafford Nye and Renata Zerkowski the Youth Movement is dismantled and the murder of the American ambassador, Mr. Cortman, is solved.

(61)   1970

NEMESIS

Some two years ago Miss Jane Marple had a holiday on the island of St. Honoré and on this island had been allies in solving a murder with Mr. Jason Rafiel, a very rich man. Miss Marple called herself Nemesis (see A Caribbean Mystery).

Now Miss Marple reads in The Times that Mr. Rafiel has died; a week later she receives through the executor of Mr. Rafiel's will a proposition to investigate a certain crime under the code word 'Nemesis'; she gets no further information, but she accepts.

A week later she gets a letter from Mr. Rafiel, written before his death, in which he suggests that she takes a seat on a tour around Britain: everything is already paid for.

During the tour she meets Miss Temple, a retired Headmistress of a girl's school, and a Professor Wanstead. Miss Temple tells her that she had a pupil, Verity Hunt, who was going to marry Michael Rafiel, the son of Jason but that Verity was murdered and Michael was convicted of the offence.

When the tour has a stop in Jocelyn St. Mary, Miss Marple is invited by the three sisters Bradbury-Scott to stay some nights in their Old Manor House; Mr. Rafiel had asked the sisters to invite Miss Marple.

During her visit Miss Marple learns that at the same time Verity was murdered another girl, Nora Broad, was reported missing, and that Verity Hunt had lived in the house of the three sisters.

During the stay in Jocelyn St. Mary, Miss Temple is murdered.

Miss Marple is getting very near to the truth, when an attempt is made to murder her.   (62)   1971

ELEPHANTS CAN REMEMBER

One day in 1972 the detective story-writer Mrs. Ariadne Oliver is visited by a Mrs. Burton-Cox who asks her to investigate the death of the parents of Celia Ravenscroft.

This girl, who is Mrs. Oliver's goddaughter, is engaged to marry Desmond, son of Mrs. Burton-Cox. Mrs. Oliver decides to consult Hercule Poirot and they both start questioning the people who knew Molly and Alistair Ravenscroft when they were still alive.

Bit by bit Mrs. Oliver and Hercule Poirot get a clearer view of the case. Celia's parents were found shot with Alistair's own revolver on the top of a cliff in Overcliffe, Cornwall. At the time a double suicide was suggested, though their marriage was said to be happy. Molly's twin sister Dolly Jarrow had been staying at Overcliffe, but died by falling from a cliff three weeks before Molly and Alistair's deaths. Mrs. Oliver and Poirot pay great attention to the fact that Molly possessed four wigs.

Dolly had suffered from a mental illness and unless she is sure that this mental flaw hasn't passed over to her, Celia will not marry Desmond. So Desmond officially asks Poirot to find out the truth. Poirot pays a visit to Dolly's mental physician, then decides to make a visit to Geneva. He visits the graves of Dolly, Molly and Alistair, and has a talk with Celia's governess, Mademoiselle Rouselle. She confirms that the Ravenscrofts were a very happy couple and points out to Poirot that he should see Mademoiselle 'Zélie' Meauchourat, who at the time of her death, was Molly's companion.

(63)   1972

Tommy and Tuppence Beresford move into a new house, The Laurels, in Hollowquay. The families, who had lived there, have left lots of children's books and Tuppence, who recognises most of them, is so attracted, that she begins to read them. In one of these books that had belonged to Alexander Parkinson, Tuppence finds a message which states that a Mary Jordan did not die naturally.

Tommy and Tuppence learn that shortly before World War I their new house was the headquarters for a group who passed secret naval plans to outsiders. British Intelligence was able to infiltrate them by giving Mary Jordan a place in the group. The discovery of this infiltration by the group led to the murder of Mary Jordan and evidently Alexander Parkinson had his suspicions.

It is clear that even sixty years after this crime, followers of the traitors want to prevent the discovery of the murder, because there is another murder and an attack on Tuppence.

With the help of old friends from British Intelligence both murders are solved.

(64)   1973

CURTAIN

For a second time Hercule Poirot and Arthur Hastings are at Styles Court. However, it is now a guest house, run by Colonel George and Mrs. Daisy Luttrell.

Poirot has gone to the guest house to catch a murderer and/or to prevent a murder, as he has discovered that five murder-cases from the past have something in common: in each case there is no doubt about the guilty person. Poirot suspects that a person X is in fact responsible for each murder; X is the perfect criminal, although X did not actively take part in the crimes. The guests at Styles are Sir William Carrington, Dr. John Franklin and his invalid wife Barbara, Hastings' daughter Judith who is Franklin's secretary, Miss Craven, the hospital nurse for Mrs. Franklin, Major Allerton, Miss Elizabeth Cole and Mr. Stephen Norton.

Poirot is sure that there will be another murder, for which X will be again responsible. There are in fact three further deaths. Very sadly one of the deaths is that of Poirot, by natural causes.

Hastings is in the dark but four months after the death of Poirot he receives from a firm of lawyers a manuscript, written by Hercule Poirot, in which he explains all the facts of the case: the second affair at Styles.

(65)   1975

Gwenda and Giles Reed, both orphans, recently married in New Zealand, are going to live in England. Gwenda goes on ahead to buy a house. She finds a house, Hillside, in Dillmouth and feels immediately at home. But she has been there before!

When Gwenda is visiting Raymond and Joan West, cousins of Giles, she is invited to see Webster's The Duchess of Malfi where she screams and leaves the theatre at the words 'Cover her face; mine eyes dazzle; she died young'. 'The words remind Gwenda of being on the stairs of a house as a three-year old girl, seeing Helen lying there, strangled. Gwenda is afraid she is mad, but Miss Marple, Raymond's aunt, reassures her that she is not. It transpires that Gwenda has indeed lived in Hillside and most probably has seen a strangled woman.

Who is Helen?

Giles and Gwenda, with the help of Miss Marple, do a lot of research. When Helen, Gwenda's stepmother, ran away, Gwenda was sent to Megan's sister Allison in New Zealand.

Miss Marple, Gwenda and Giles doubt whether Helen ran away, and together find the truth.

(66)   1976

THE
SHORT STORIES

Hercule Poirot is approached by Lady Yardly and Mary Marvell who are anxious to discover the source of several menacing letters which Mary has received.

It transpires that some years ago Lady Yardly was given a present; "The Star of the East" diamond, by her husband Lord Yardly. However, after an affair she succumbed to blackmail and as a result parted with the diamond, replacing it with a paste replica to deceive her husband. It is this same diamond which Mary Marvell is given at her wedding, except under the new name of "The Western Star".

Complications arise when Lady Yardly discovers that her husband wishes to sell the diamond which they own, unaware that it is a paste replica, and as a result she finds it necessary to turn to Gregory Rolf, Mary Marvell's husband for help.

(67)   1924

THE TRAGEDY AT
MARSDON MANOR

Hercule is asked by his friend Alfred Wright to investigate the ostensibly natural death of Mr. Maltravers of Marsdon Manor, Essex. The doctor, Dr. Ralph Bernard had attributed the cause of death to a haemorrhage, but Alfred Wright suspects otherwise.

The reason for Alfred Wright's interest in the case is the fact that Mr. Maltravers' life was insured for £50,000 and as a director of the company which issued the policy; The Northern Union Insurance Company, he is anxious to determine whether any foul play was involved.

(68)   1924

THE ADVENTURE OF THE CHEAP FLAT

During the course of a small soirée Captain Hastings, a friend of Hercule Poirot is entertained with the story of a Mr. and Mrs. Robinson's incredible luck in their house-hunting endeavours. Hastings finds the fact that the couple had the enviable luck of renting a flat at Montague Mansions, Knightsbridge for £80 per annum rather than the customary £350 very intriguing and tells Poirot.

Poirot also finds it an intriguing tale, and having no other cases to pursue attempts to unravel the apparent mystery behind it.

(69)   1924

Mr. Roger Havering of Hunter's Lodge, Derbyshire visits Poirot in an attempt to persuade him to undertake a case. He has recently received a telegram from his wife informing him that his uncle, Mr. Harrington Pace has been murdered.

Poirot is unable to undertake the case personally as he is indisposed with influenza, but he allows Captain Hastings to accompany Roger Havering to Derbyshire, on the condition that he is kept constantly informed.

When Mr. Havering and Hastings reach Hunter's Lodge, Inspector Japp of Scotland Yard is already there. Together they learn from Mrs. Zoe Havering and the housekeeper, Mrs. Middleton, that a stranger visited the late Mr. Pace the night before and left through a window.

(70)   1924

THE MILLION DOLLAR
BOND ROBBERY

Poirot is asked by Miss Esmée Farquhar to assist her fiancé Philip Ridgeway who is under suspicion of theft.

Mr. Ridgeway, an employee of the London and Scottish Bank was put in charge of ensuring that over one million dollars in Liberty Bonds reached New York safely. They were locked in his trunk on board the ship "Olympia", however, shortly before the ship reached New York it was discovered that the bonds had been stolen.

During his investigation Poirot discovers that only 3 men had a key to the trunk on board the ship; Philip Ridgeway, and the two general managers of the Bank, Philip's uncle, Mr. Vavasour, and Mr. Shaw.

(71)   1924

THE ADVENTURES OF THE EGYPTIAN TOMB

Sir John Willard, an archaeologist, and Mr Bleibner, a wealthy amateur discover near Cairo the tomb of King Men-her-Ra. Within a month of this discovery Sir John Willard dies of heart failure, Mr Bleibner dies of blood poisoning, and his nephew in New York, Rupert Bleibner shoots himself.

Poirot is asked by Lady Willard to investigate these deaths in an attempt to protect her son, Sir Guy Willard, and subsequently Poirot and Captain Hastings travel to Egypt to investigate.

On arriving in Cairo they are faced with a new development — the death of Mr Schneider of the Metropolitan Museum from tetanus.

(72)   1924

THE JEWEL ROBBERY AT THE "GRAND METROPOLITAN"

During a weekend at the Grand Metropolitan Hotel in Brighton, Poirot and Captain Hastings become acquainted with Mr Ed Opalsen, an oil baron, and his wife.

Poirot is presented with a case to solve when Mrs Opalsen, anxious to show him her jewels discovers that her pearl necklace, which she had left in her room has been stolen. The two suspects in the case, the hotel chambermaid, and Mrs Opalsen's maid Célestine are searched, but nothing is found.

(73)   1924

THE
KIDNAPPED PRIME MINISTER

During the first World War, Poirot and Captain Hastings are informed by the Leader of the House of Commons and a member of the War Cabinet that the Prime Minister, David MacAdam, has been kidnapped.

Having survived an earlier assassination attempt the Prime Minister has been kidnapped somewhere between Boulogne and Paris, whilst on a visit to France. His secretary, Captain Daniels, has been found chloroformed in France, and his chauffeur O'Murphy is known to have disappeared somewhere in London.

(74)   1924

THE DISAPPEARANCE OF
MR DAVENHEIM

Inspector Japp of Scotland Yard bets Poirot £5 that he cannot solve the case of the disappearance of Mr Davenheim without moving from his chair.

Mr Davenheim, a senior partner of the bankers Davenheim and Salmon tells his wife that he is going into the village where they live, and if Mr Lowen, a business acquaintance, should arrive could he wait. However Mr Davenheim never returns.

Further developments occur when the Davenheim's safe is robbed, the clothes which Mr Davenheim wore when he disappeared are found, and his ring is pawned in London by a man called Billy Kellet, already well-known to the police.

(75)   1924

THE ADVENTURE OF THE
ITALIAN NOBLEMAN

On the invitation of Dr. Hawker, Poirot investigates the death of Count Foscatini of Regent's Court.

While visiting Poirot, Dr. Hawker is informed by his terrified housekeeper that there has been a telephone call for him in which a man identifying himself as Foscatini said he had been killed.

On arriving at Foscatini's flat they find that he has been killed by a blow on the head, and in the room are the remains of a meal for three.

(76)   1924

Miss Violet Marsh, an orphan, is treated by her uncle, Andrew Marsh of Crabtree Manor, Devonshire as his own daughter.

However, they disagree over the question of education for Violet, and when he dies Andrew Marsh's will leaves Crabtree Manor to Violet for one year only, in which time she must prove that her wits are better than his.

In an attempt to do so she calls in Poirot to assist her.

(77)   1924

A FAIRY ON THE FLAT

Some years after World War One, Mr and Mrs Beresford, alias Tommy and Tuppence are visited by Mr Carter, Chief of Intelligence.

The object of his visit is to persuade them to undertake the running of the International Detective Agency for six months, paying particular attention to any letters they may receive which bear a Russian stamp with the number 16 written underneath. Tommy and Tuppence agree to this proposition on the condition that they are free to run the agency as they please.

Remark   This story introduces a collection of stories entitled "Partners in Crime". In these 15 stories Tommy plays the role of Theodore Blunt, and Tuppence that of his confidential secretary Miss Robinson.

Remark   Throughout the course of this collection of stories Tommy and Tuppence impersonate a variety of famous people, including Sherlock Holmes, Dr Fortune, Superintendent Bell, Poirot and Hastings.

Remark   The title of this story is derived from the fact that a scratch upon a photograph resembled a fairy.

(78)   1929

A POT OF TEA

Thomas Beresford acting as the manager of "Blunt's Brilliant Detectives" is approached by a new client, Lawrence St. Vincent.

St. Vincent has come to the Detective Agency in an attempt to discover the whereabouts of Jeanette Smith, an employee of Madame Violettes' Hat Shop, who has suddenly disappeared.

(79)   1929

THE AFFAIR OF THE PINK PEARL

During an evening at the Laurels guest house in Wimbledon, run by Colonel Kingston Bruce and his wife, a pink pearl belonging to one of the guests — Mrs Hamilton Betts, is lost.

Remembering a story told to her by Lawrence St. Vincent ("A Pot of Tea"), Beatrice Kingston Bruce, anxious to help her parents, seeks help from the International Detective Agency, run by Tommy and Tuppence.

(80)   1929

THE ADVENTURE OF THE SINISTER STRANGER

This adventure begins with the arrival at the International Detective Agency of a letter bearing a Russian stamp.

Tommy Beresford soon discovers that the letter is of considerable interest to several people, including one man calling himself Detective Inspector Dymchurch. Having told these interested parties that Tuppence is in possession of the letter which they desire, Tommy finds himself forced to write to her.

(81)   1929

Tommy and Tuppence whilst reading the "Daily Leader" are intrigued by the fact that on different days of the week white dots appear in different positions in the headlines. They also come across an interesting advertisement. "I should go three hearts. 12 tricks. Ace of spades. Necessary to finesse the king", which Tuppence succeeds in interpreting. Her deduction is that the advert refers to something which will happen at 12 o'clock at the Three Acts Ball in the underground den – the Ace of Spades.

On arriving at the costume ball Tommy and Tuppence discover that one of the guests dressed as the Queen of Hearts has been stabbed to death, and that she died clutching a piece of newspaper and gasping the words, "Bingo did it – ."

(82)   1929

110

THE CASE OF THE MISSING LADY

Tommy Beresford acting as Mr. Theodore Blunt, manager of the International Detective Agency is asked by Mr. Gabriel Staransson to find his fiancée Hermione Crane who has mysteriously disappeared.

Miss Crane lives with her aunt, Lady Susan Clonray in Pont Street but she is unwilling to impart any information about the whereabouts of her niece.

(83)   1929

During this case Tommy acting as Theodore Blunt, adopts the guise of a blind man, and relies upon Tuppence to lead him.

While they are lunching at the Blitz they are approached by the Duke of Blairgowrie and a man named Captain Harper who inform them that the Duke's daughter has been abducted. Tommy returns to the Duke's home, without Tuppence to pursue the case further, only to find that he has been duped and the man professing to be the Duke intends to kill him.

(84)   1929

THE MAN IN THE MIST

During the course of this particular case Tommy dons the disguise of a Roman Catholic priest.

Whilst enjoying cocktails at the Grand Adlington Hotel, Tommy and Tuppence meet Marvyn Estcourt, and the actress Miss Gilda Glen, who is shortly to be married to Lord Leconbury.

Having been asked by Miss Glen to meet her at The White House in Morgan's Avenue, Tommy and Tuppence make their way there passing on the way, James Reilly a devoted admirer of Miss Glen's, in the company of a policeman. When they reach The White House belonging to Miss Glen's sister they discover that Gilda has been murdered. Reilly is arrested as the murderer.

(85)   1929

THE CRACKLER

In this instance Tommy and Tuppence are asked by Inspector Marriot to help him round up a gang of counterfeiters. His suspects in this criminal intrigue are, Major Laidlaw, his French wife Marguerite, and her father M. Heroulde.

In their attempt to assist Inspector Marriot, Tommy and Tuppence use their contact Lawrence St. Vincent to infiltrate the rich social set in which these characters mix, and as a result they also meet Jimmy Faulkener and Hank Ryder from Alabama.

(86)   1929

THE SUNNINGDALE MYSTERY

While having lunch Tommy and Tuppence discuss the Sunningdale murder mystery which they have just read about in the "Daily Leader".

The information revealed in the newspaper is that on the seventh tee of the Sunningdale golf course a certain Captain Sessle was found dead – stabbed in the heart with a hat pin. Subsequent inquiries have revealed that Mr Hollaby, a friend, and a partner of Captain Sessle in the Porcupine Assurance company, was playing golf with him the day before. Hollaby remembers that he witnessed Sessle leave the sixth tee with a woman for a few minutes, and then excuse himself to go home at the eighth tee after playing a disastrous couple of holes. The next day he was found dead at the seventh tee with some tell-tale hair and woolthreads in his hand. A woman – Doris Evans has been arrested for the murder of Captain Sessle, after admitting to the police that she had a fight with him.

(87)   1929

Tommy and Tuppence in their guises as Theodore Blunt and Miss Robinson of the International Detective Agency, are approached by Miss Lois Hargreaves.

Miss Hargreaves has come to them for help after discovering that the occupants of her house, Thurnly Grange have been made ill by a box of chocolates containing arsenic. She goes on to inform Tommy and Tuppence that the house was left to her by her Aunt, Lucy Radclyffe and that the other occupants are; Captain Dennis Radclyffe who will inherit the house upon her death, Miss Logan a former companion of Lucy Radclyffe and Mary Chilcott an old schoolfriend of Lois.

Tommy and Tuppence agree to undertake the case and travel down to Thurnly Grange only to discover that Lois and Dennis are dead and that Miss Logan is seriously ill.

(88)   1929

THE UNBREAKABLE ALIBI

Tommy and Tuppence are asked by Mr. Montgomery Jones to help him win a bet which he has made with Miss Una Drake.

Miss Drake formerly from Australia, and now living in London bet Mr. Montgomery Jones that she could produce an unshakeable alibi, and that if by any chance he should succeed in proving it to be untrue he could ask her to marry him. She then proved to Mr. Montgomery Jones that she was in both Torquay and London at the same time.

It is in an attempt to prove that this is untrue that Mr. Montgomery Jones has approached the International Detective Agency.

(89)   1929

THE CLERGYMAN'S DAUGHTER AND THE RED HOUSE

Miss Monica Dean approaches the International Detective Agency run by Tommy and Tuppence after her suspicions have been aroused by strange occurrences in her home, and by two men in particular.

Miss Dean lives with her sick mother in the Red House at Stourton-in-the-Marsh, which was left to her by a rich aunt when she died. Miss Dean informs Tommy and Tuppence that she has recently been approached by two men wanting to buy the house — a young gentleman, and an older man, Dr. O'Neill of the "Society for Physical Research", whom she suspects are the same person. She is also anxious to discover the cause of strange events which began to occur in the house after the visit of the young gentleman, and which resulted in her paying guests leaving.

(90)   1929

THE AMBASSADOR'S BOOTS

Mr. Randolph Wilmott, United States Ambassador to the Court of St. James asks Tommy acting as Theodore Blunt of the International Detective Agency to solve the puzzle of the confusion over the kitbag containing his boots.

On arriving in England he found himself in possession of someone else's kitbag bearing the same initials as his; RW, and believed it to belong to Ralph Westerham, a United States senator. Some hours after their arrival someone calling himself Westerham's valet came and exchanged the kitbags. However the Ambassador is suspicious about the whole affair.

(91)   1929

119

Mr. Carter, Chief of Intelligence and the man responsible for persuading Tommy and Tuppence to run the International Detective Agency for six months, gives them special instructions concerning the impending arrival of a Russian agent. This agent is the man responsible for despatching certain letters to England with the number 16 written under the stamp.

Tommy and Tuppence alias Theodore Blunt and Miss Robinson are then visited by Prince Vladiroffsky, and later he takes Tuppence out to lunch at the Blitz, where he is staying. After lunch he takes her up to room 318 where she meets Mrs. Cortlandt Van Snyder from Detroit. Carter and Tommy meanwhile are searching for a man named De Vareze who they believe to be the Russian agent who has recently arrived in England.

(92)   1929

THE COMING OF MR. QUIN

During a New Year's Eve celebration held by Tom and Lady Laura Evesham, the conversation turns to a discussion about the man who previously owned the house, Mr. Derek Capel, who shot himself.

The participants in this conversation are the host and hostess, Sir Richard Conway, Alex and Eleanor Portal, and Mr. Satterthwaite. Laura and Eleanor retire to bed, and the discussion takes an unexpected turn when a stranger who has recently been involved in a car accident arrives at the house. This stranger, Mr. Harley Quin has some added information to tell those assembled about the death of Mr. Derek Capel.

While Eleanor listens in the gallery above, Mr Harley Quin tells them about how Mr. Capel came to shoot himself. After reading in a newspaper about the imminent exhumation of the body of a man named Appleton, whose wife was accused of poisoning him but was acquitted, Mr. Capel saw a policeman outside his home, and shot himself. Mr. Harley Quin explains that Capel loved Appleton's wife and poisoned Appleton with strychnine dissolved in port. However, Mrs. Appleton broke the decanter containing the port, destroyed the evidence and allowed herself to be tried for the crime.

(93)   1930

121

Mr. and Mrs. Onkerton of Greenways House invite friends to stay with them. Among the guests are Lady Cynthia Drage, Richard Scott and his wife Moira, Major John Porter, Iris Staverton, Captain Jimmy Allenson and Mr. Satterthwaite.

The house in which they are staying is reputed to be haunted by a ghost; a murdered cavalier is said to have been seen looking through the window of a certain room, and it is in this room that the Scotts are placed. The mystery thickens when Jimmy Allenson and Moira Scott are found shot dead. It is later revealed that they were killed by the same shot, and that another bullet missed them and hit Moira's earring.

(94)   1930

After being involved in a car accident near Kirtlington Mallet, Mr. Satterthwaite goes to a local inn, the "Bells and Motley" for a meal. While there he meets Mr. Harley Quin, and a conversation begins between these two men and the landlord William Jones who informs them about the disappearance of Captain Richard Hartwell.

The landlord informs them that Captain Hartwell disappeared 3 months ago, and that the last person to see him was his gardener John Mathias. Captain Hartwell had only recently been married to Miss Eleanor le Couteau, the owner of Ashley Grange. After the disappearance of Captain Hartwell, Eleanor, with the assistance of her companion Mrs. St. Clair sold everything to Mr. Cyrus G. Bradburn and went abroad.

(95)   1930

Mr. Satterthwaite and Mr. Quin attempt to solve the murder of Lady Vivien Barnaby, wife of Sir George Barnaby of Deering Hall.

The information available about the case is that Lady Vivien was shot dead on Friday 13th and that the shots were heard at 6.20. A man named Martin Wylde has been arrested for the murder after admitting leaving his gun at Deering Hall when he left there at about 6.25 on Friday 13th.

In an attempt to uncover the truth Mr. Satterthwaite goes to Banff in Canada to interview Louisa Bullard, the housemaid at Deering Hall when the murder was committed. Louisa assists Quin and Satterthwaite in their efforts by informing them that she heard a train go past shortly before she heard the fatal shots which killed Lady Vivien.

Remark   The title of the story comes from the fact that Louisa saw a gigantic hand in the smoke left by the passing train.

(96)   1930

While at a casino in Monte Carlo, Satterthwaite becomes acquainted with the Countess Czarnova and two Americans, Franklin Rudge and Elizabeth Martin. Elizabeth is in love with Frank, but he in turn is captivated by the Countess.

While they are gambling Satterthwaite wins but the croupier gives his winnings to the Countess. Later, after Mr. Harley Quin has arrived, the croupier, Pierre Vauchier explains the reasons for his actions.

(97)   1930

THE MAN FROM THE SEA

Whilst spending some time on a small Spanish island, Satterthwaite succeeds in saving two people from committing suicide.

Near a villa called La Paz he meets Anthony Cosden, a man who is considering suicide because the doctors have given him only 6 months to live. He reveals to Satterthwaite that the evening before another man called Mr. Harley Quin prevented him from committing suicide, but that the only thing which could really save him would be if he had a son.

Satterthwaite then meets a woman, who, like Anthony Cosden is considering suicide. Her son whom she gave birth to after a love affair 20 years ago is about to get married, and she cannot bring herself to tell him who his father is.

(98)   1930

THE VOICE IN THE DARK

Mr. Satterthwaite is asked for help by Lady Beatrice Stranleigh who is concerned about her daughter Margery. It appears that Margery has been hearing voices at night telling her to "give back what is not yours".

After this meeting in Cannes, Mr. Satterthwaite returns to England where he goes to Lady Stranleigh's estate in Wiltshire — Abbot's Mede. Whilst making this journey he meets Mr. Harley Quin who is staying near the estate at the "Bells and Motley". Satterthwaite tells Quin that Lady Barbara Stranleigh had an elder sister, Beatrice, who was drowned, while Barbara and their maid Alice Clayton survived. Together Satterthwaite and Quin attempt to unravel the truth behind the voices Lady Stranleigh's daughter has been hearing.

(99)   1930

Whilst at the opera Mr. Satterthwaite and Mr. Harley Quinn are attracted by the beautiful face of another member of the audience, Gillian West. Miss West is sitting with two men; Mr. Philip Eastney and Mr. Charles Burns and when a fight breaks out between them it is Mr. Satterthwaite who sees Gillian safely home.

The next day Gillian West and Charles Burns announce their engagement. As a wedding present from Philip, Gillian receives a wireless set and a glass beaker, and upon his request promises to listen to a certain concert that evening. Satterthwaite meets Philip at the Arlecchio restaurant later and discovers that Gillian's life is in danger.

(100)   1930

THE DEAD HARLEQUIN

The purchase of a painting entitled The Dead Harlequin by Frank Bristow results in Satterthwaite and Quin being presented with another mystery to solve. The painting set in the Terrace Room at Charnley depicts a harlequin lying dead on the ground and another looking through the window. Satterthwaite's reason for buying the painting is that it reminds him of his friend, Mr. Harley Quin.

During a subsequent dinner party at which the artist Bristow, and a certain Colonel Mouchton are present, the conversation turns to Charnley, the scene of the painting. They discuss the suicide of Lord Reggie Charnley fourteen years ago in the Oak parlour at Charnley. Colonel Mouchton was there at the time and remembers that Lord Charnley's widow, Alix Charnley went abroad and shortly after gave birth to a son, Dick, who inherited the title.

Later Satterthwaite is asked first by an actress Aspasia Glen, and then by Alix Charnley to sell the painting. Satterthwaite agrees to sell it to Mrs. Charnley, although he is still intrigued by the death of her husband.

(101)   1930

THE BIRD WITH THE BROKEN WING

Satterthwaite goes to a houseparty outside London, having declined an invitation to dinner with the Keeleys at Laidell. However, whilst at this party those assembled play "table turning", and Satterthwaite receives a message: QUIN and LAIDELL, and after excusing himself travels to Laidell.

At this dinner party the host and hostess are David Keeley and his daughter, Madge. The assembled guests include Satterthwaite, Doris Coles, Mrs. Graham and her son Roger, Gerard Annesley and Mabelle Annesley-Clydesley. Mabelle entertains the guests by playing her ukelele, and the title of the story is derived from the fact that Satterthwaite calls her, "The bird with the broken wing". Later in the evening she retires taking her ukelele with her, and in the morning she is found to have hung herself.

(102)   1930

THE WORLD'S END

During a visit to Corsica with the Duchess of Leith, Satterthwaite meets Naomi Carlton Smith, a painter, and Mr. Tomlinson, a retired Indian judge. Together they go sightseeing at a village called Cotichiaveeri which Naomi calls "World's End". While there they meet Mr. Harley Quin, and later whilst in Carsecroute they meet Mr. Vyse, a producer, the actress Rosina Nunn and her husband Henry Judge.

During the course of a conversation Rosina Nunn tells the assembled company about an opal she once possessed which was stolen. It transpires that a playwright, Alec Gerard is in jail being punished for the crime. The tale takes an unexpected twist when the opal is found in an Indian box, and Alec Gerard, who is engaged to Naomi Carlton-Smith is freed, thus preventing Naomi from committing suicide.

(103)   1930

HARLEQUIN'S LANE

Both Satterthwaite and Mr Harley Quin become involved in a harlequinade which John and Anna Denman are planning to hold at their house, "Ashmead".

Satterthwaite meets Quin while he is walking through Harlequin Lane, and subsequently both men become involved in helping to plan the harlequinade. Molly Stanwell is to play the pierrette and Mr Marly the pierrot, while two professionals will play Harlequin and Columbine.

During the planning Claude Wickam who is responsible for the music speaks about a great Russian dancer, Madame Kharsanova who is now dead. Complications arise when Prince Serquis Oranoff who is supposed to be bringing the professionals to "Ashmead" is involved in an accident. As a result Anna Denman has to play Columbine, and Mr Quin the Harlequin.

After the harlequinade Anna Denman dies.

(104)   1930

THE TUESDAY NIGHT CLUB

Six people join together to form a club — The Tuesday Night Club. They plan to meet every Tuesday and each member in turn will be expected to propound a problem for the other members to solve. The members of this exclusive club are; Raymond West a writer; Joyce Lemprière an artist; Sir Henry Clithering a retired commissioner of Scotland Yard; Dr Pender a clergyman; Mr Petherick a solicitor and Miss Jane Marple.

The first problem is put forward by Sir Henry. He tells the other members of the club the story of a supper one year ago after which two of the diners became very ill and one died. The people involved were Mr and Mrs Albert Jones and Miss Milly Clark. All three ate tinned lobster and trifle with hundreds and thousands, and afterwards Mrs Jones died.

(105)   1932

Dr Pender presents the other members of the Tuesday Club with another problem to solve. He tells them the tale of Sir Richard Haydon the owner of "Silent Grove" in Dartmoor.

Shortly after he had bought the house Sir Richard invited guests to stay with him. Among the guests were his cousin Elliot Haydon, Lady Mannering and her daughter Violet, Captain Rogers and his wife, Dr Symonds and Miss Diana Ashley. Richard showed the guests over his estate, showing them in particular some old relics, and the ancient grove of Astarte.

Whilst in the grove Diana played the part of Astarte, as she was doing so Richard moved towards her and stumbled. When Elliot turned Richard over they discovered that he was dead, and that although he had been stabbed there was no weapon.

(106)   1932

Raymond West is the next member of the Tuesday Club to present his problem to the others.

He tells them of his Whitsun visit to John Newman in Polperran, Cornwall, and about the fact that Newman was particularly interested in a shipwreck reputed to contain gold which was lying on the Serpent Rocks.

West tells the other members of the club that whilst travelling on the train to Polperran he met Inspector Badgworth, who regaled him with a tale about the shipwreck of a ship named Otranto and the bullion which went missing from it. On arriving in Polperran it was discovered that Newman had disappeared. However he was soon found and claimed that he had been tied up by the gold robbers after witnessing the theft from the Otranto. Once freed he also implicated Mr Kelvin, the landlord of the "Three Anchors" in the crime.

(107)   1932

Joyce Lemprière tells the other members of the Tuesday Club about something which she experienced whilst staying at "The Polharwith Arms" five years ago.

Another of the guests Captain Denis Dacre met an old acquaintance, Miss Carol Harding and introduced her to his wife, Margery. All three planned to go bathing, Denis Dacre and his wife went by boat, and Miss Harding set off on foot. As time wore on Carol Harding did not return, and after making some inquiries Denis Dacre and his wife left the hotel. Some time later Carol Harding returned and Joyce read in a newspaper that Mrs Dacre had been drowned.

Remark   The title of the story is derived from the fact that Joyce saw blood dripping from the red bathing suit onto the pavement.

(108)   1932

Mr Petherick tells the assembled members of the Tuesday Club about an incident involving one of his clients.

After the death of his brother, Mr Simon Clode adopted his brother's three children, George, Grace and Mary. He provided for them all equally in his will, however with the appearance of Mrs Eurydice Spragg everything was altered. Mrs Spragg was a spiritualist, and after meeting her Mr Clode altered his will naming her as the main benefactor. This new will was witnessed by Emma Gaunt, the housemaid and Lucy David, the cook, and was sealed in a blue envelope. However when the envelope was opened upon Mr Clode's death all it contained was a sheet of blank paper.

(109)   1932

THE THUMB MARK OF ST. PETER

Miss Marple tells the assembled company about the murder of her neice Mabel's husband, Geoffrey Denham which occurred 15 years ago.

Mabel and Geoffrey lived at "Myrtles Dene" with Geoffrey's father who was ill and afflicted by a streak of insanity which ran in the family. When Geoffrey was found dead Mabel was accused of the murder and in desperation turned to her aunt Jane for help.

(110)   1932

Colonel Arthur Bantry and his wife Dolly invite Sir Henry Clithering, Miss Marple, Dr Lloyd and Jane Helier to dinner. During the course of the dinner the Colonel tells them a curious tale of George and Mary Pritchard.

Mary was an invalid, nursed by Miss Copling. She had a great weakness for fortune tellers and was told by Zarida, the Psychic Reader of the Fortune to beware of blue flowers. This warning was proved to have been in earnest when a primrose, a hollyhock and a geranium on Mary's wallpaper all turned blue, and shortly afterwards she died.

(111)   1932

THE COMPANION

During a dinner given by Colonel Arthur and Mrs Dolly Bantry for Jane Helier, Miss Marple and Sir Henry Clithering, another of the guests, Dr Lloyd tells them about an experience he had in Las Palmas some years ago.

While staying in Las Palmas he observed two English ladies, Miss Mary Barton and her companion Miss Amy Durant. On one particular occasion the two ladies went to the beach after having decided to go bathing. Whilst bathing Amy was drowned and Mary was saved. However Dr Lloyd was dissatisfied and his suspicions were fuelled by a Spanish woman's insistence that Mary had drowned Amy. The mystery deepened when some months later Mary Barton was reported to have drowned herself in Cornwall, but the body was never found.

(112)   1932

THE FOUR SUSPECTS

At a dinner given by Colonel and Mrs. Bantry, Sir Henry Clithering seizes the opportunity to tell the assembled guests about an unsolved crime.

He tells them about a man named Dr. Rosen who succeeded in infiltrating a German secret society called the Schwarze Hand, which was involved in blackmail and terrorism. After doing so he travelled to England where he settled in a cottage in Somerset. With him lived his niece Greta Rosen, his secretary Charles Templeton, his servant Mrs. Gertrud Schwartz and the gardener Dobbs.

While living in England Dr. Rosen fell down a flight of stairs and broke his neck. All the other members of the household were under suspicion, and particular concern was placed upon the fact that his death might have been some form of retribution from the Schwarze Hand. In addition to these suspicions it was known that shortly before his death Dr. Rosen had received a letter mentioning Dr. Helmuth Spath, Edgar Jackson, Amos Perry, Tsington and Honesty (D.E.A.T.H.)

(113)   1932

A CHRISTMAS TRAGEDY

Miss Marple tells Colonel and Mrs. Bantry's guests about a tragedy which occurred shortly before Christmas some years ago.

While staying at the Grand Spa Hotel she met Jack and Gladys Sanders. After forseeing that Jack intended to murder his wife Miss Marple laid a trap for him, but he successfully avoided it and almost succeeded in carrying out the perfect murder.

One evening Miss Marple went upstairs with Jack and found Gladys dead. Miss Marple realised that Jack had an alibi but when they returned to look at the body with an Inspector she noticed that the ear-clips which were on the body had disappeared, as had a hat.

(114)   1932

142

THE HERB OF DEATH

In the company of her husband and their guests Mrs. Bantry takes the opportunity to tell her tale.

She tells them about the fatal consequences of a dinner which she and Arthur attended at Clodderham Court. Among the other guests were Sylvia Keene, Maud Wye, Mr. Curle, Mrs. Adelaide Carpenter and Jerry Lorimer, and they were all the guests of Ambrose Beray. For their meal they all ate duck with sage stuffing and afterwards all the guests became very ill and Sylvia died.

Later examination showed that the sage had been mixed with foxglove leaves, and suspicion fell upon Jerry, Sylvia's fiancé who married Maud only 6 months after Sylvia's death.

(115)   1932

THE AFFAIR AT THE BUNGALOW

Jane Helier takes the opportunity to tell a story about an experience she had whilst staying at the Bridge Hotel with her understudy Netta Green, during rehearsals for the play, "Smith" by Somerset Maugham.

Jane was called to the police station to meet Mr. Leslie Faulkener, a playwright who claimed to know her, but when they came face to face neither of them recognised the other. Leslie claimed that he had been called to the Bungalow owned by Sir Herman Cohen to meet Miss Helier and discuss a play. He remembered being given a cocktail and then waking up on the road and being arrested by the police in connection with a burglary at the bungalow.

Miss Helier tells the Bantry's guests that it became obvious that someone had lured her from the bungalow and put an impostor in her place to meet Leslie and drug him. Someone also contacted Miss Mary Kerr, a woman who often spent weekends at the bungalow with Sir Herman Cohen and told her about the robbery. However this is all that anyone can deduce about the mystery and none of the Bantry's guests are any more successful in shedding any light upon the mysterious events.

(116)   1932

DEATH BY DROWNING

While staying with the Bantry's, Sir Henry Clithering is visited by Miss Marple who asks for his help in solving a case.

She informs him that Rose Emmott, daughter of Tom Emmott the landlord of the Blue Boar has drowned herself after becoming involved with a man named Rex Sandford. In addition to this Miss Marple also tells Sir Henry that before her involvement with Rex Sandford, Rose Emmott had been close to Joe Ellis. Miss Marple suspects that a murder has been committed, and with this in mind Sir Henry sets about investigating the case.

(117)   1932

Before leaving London to stay with his sister Kitty in Cornwall, Mr. Anstruther meets an American correspondent called William P. Ryan who tells him an intriguing tale.

He tells Mr. Anstruther how, at the beginning of the first world war a large convent in a village in Belgium blew up the moment the Germans came in. The explosion was attributed to the supernatural powers of one of the nuns, and on one of the few standing walls left the black shape of a hound was found.

Anstruther is intrigued to learn that this nun became a refugee and now lives in the same village in Cornwall as his sister. His sister Kitty informs him that the nun's name is Sister Marie Angelique and that the local doctor, Dr. Rose keeps her under close observation.

On returning to London, Anstruther learns that Dr. Rose and Sister Marie Angelique have been killed. They were killed when Dr. Rose's cottage was demolished in a landslide which left a pile of debris in the shape of a hound. It also transpires that Dr. Rose's uncle died at the same time and left everything to his nephew.

(118)   1933

146

THE RED SIGNAL

Mr. Jack Trent and his wife Claire decide to hold a dinner party for some friends. Among the guests are Mrs. Violet Eversleigh, Sir Alington West a Harley Street expert on mental disease, and his nephew Dermot West.

During the dinner Violet chooses to discuss premonition and intuition, while Dermot talks about green and red signals, and the fact that he is feeling a red signal. Later, during an after dinner séance conducted by the medium Mrs. Thompson it is revealed that one of the men should not go home. After the séance the guests all go to the Grafton Galleries to dance. However, Alington takes Dermot home for a short while and informs him that although he may love Claire she cannot divorce Jack.

Later Alington is found shot dead, and Dermot is the most obvious suspect.

(119)   1933

147

THE FOURTH MAN

By sheer coincidence Canon Parfitt of Bradchester, Sir George Durand a famous lawyer, and Dr. Campbell Clark a mental specialist find themselves in the same first-class carriage of a train travelling from London to Newcastle.

As the journey continues the three men begin to discuss the classic case of a split personality, oblivious of the presence of a fourth man in the carriage. They discuss the case of Felicie Bault. Felicie was put in to a home in Brittany when she was five, and when she was twenty-two a strange phenomena occurred. Her personality became fragmented until there were four clearly separate personalities within her. Felicie 1 was stupid and lazy; Felicie 2 was intelligent and pleasant; Felicie 3 was intelligent and pleasant but morally depraved and Felicie 4 was dreamy. Finally, after some years Felicie died in strange circumstances.

At this point the fourth man in the carriage, Raoul Letardean, interjects with some intriguing information about Felicie's condition, and her death. He informs them of a woman named Annette Ravel who made Felicie her slave and succeeded in hypnotising her. Annette, who was a singer, left the home for some time but returned to die, yet even in death she had an effect upon Felicie.

(120)   1933

THE GIPSY

After his fiancée Esther has broken off their engagement Dickie Carpenter goes to visit his friend Macfarlane who is engaged to Rachel Lawes.

During a conversation with Macfarlane, Dickie tells him about an aversion he has to gipsies and about a recent dream he has had. He dreamt that he saw Mrs. Alistair Haworth-Ferguesson as a gipsy, and bearing this in mind Macfarlane goes to visit Mrs. Haworth-Ferguesson after Dickie's sudden death.

(121)   1933

THE LAMP

A widow named Mrs. Lancaster buys a house in Weyminster for herself, her son Geoffrey and her father Mr. Winburn, even though she is aware that the house is reputed to be haunted.

When they buy the house the estate agent, Mr. Raddish tells them of the events of 30 years ago which led to the house being branded as haunted. The occupants at that time were a man named Williams and his son. When the police tried to arrest him Mr. Williams shot himself and his son starved to death in the house.

As time goes on both Mr Winburn and Geoffrey hear footsteps and sobbing, but Mrs. Lancaster remains sceptical even when Geoffrey insists that he has seen a child in the house. However, Mrs. Lancaster becomes less sceptical when Geoffrey dies and she hears two pairs of footsteps walking about the house.

(122)   1933

WIRELESS

Mrs. Mary Harter, a widow, is told by her doctor, Dr. Meynell that she must avoid all excitement because of her cardiac complaint. Hoping to make his aunt's life more pleasant, her nephew Charles Ridgeway installs a wireless set for her to listen to.

However, while listening to the wireless Mary hears the voice of her late husband Patrick telling her; "I am coming to you soon". Following this Patrick does indeed appear before Mary one Friday evening, but the excitement proves to be too much for her and she dies.

Remark   Alternative title
Where There's a Will

(123)   1933

THE WITNESS FOR THE PROSECUTION

This case is concerned with the fate of one Leonard Vole who has been charged with the murder of Miss Emily French. Miss French's maid is convinced that Leonard, who was the principal beneficiary upon Emily French's death is guilty. His predicament is made worse by the fact that his wife Romaine refuses to corroborate his alibi.

Things become more complicated when it transpires that Romaine is not in fact his wife but is already married to someone in Austria. However, Leonard's lawyer Mr. Maykerne receives help in defending his client when he is told to go to 16 Shaw's Rents in Stepney. Once there he meets a woman called Mrs. Mogson who gives him letters from Romaine to a man named Max which prove that Romaine was lying when she said Leonard was not with her on the night of the murder.

Subsequently Leonard Vole is acquitted from the charge of murder but not by totally ethical means.

(124)   1933

THE MYSTERY OF THE BLUE JAR

After hearing a woman's voice crying "Help! Murder!" from a nearby cottage Jack Hartington visits the girl who lives there. Felice Marchand says that she has heard nothing and fearing that he has been suffering from hallucinations Jack consults Dr. Ambrose Lavington.

Lavington discovers that a couple named Turner used to live in the cottage and that after leaving the cottage no trace of Mrs. Turner was ever found again. After this revelation Felice admits that she has had dreams in which a lady with a blue china jar cries for help.

In an attempt to solve this mystery Jack borrows a blue china jar belonging to his uncle George and goes to spend the night in the cottage with Felice and Lavington. However, after drinking some coffee, Jack falls asleep and when he wakes up Felice, Lavington and the jar have disappeared.

(125)   1933

THE STRANGE CASE OF
SIR ARTHUR CARMICHAEL

This story is taken from a series of notes written by the late psychologist Dr. Edward Carstairs, M.D.

In these notes he mentions a curious visit he made to the home of the Carmichael family in Wolden, on the request of Dr. Settie. He was informed that the late Sir William Carmichael had married twice, and that he had two sons, Arthur now 23 years old, from his first marriage, and an eight year old son from his second marriage to an oriental lady.

The purpose of his visit was to investigate the cause of a sudden bout of lunacy which had descended upon Arthur making him behave like a cat. Things became more mysterious when Carstairs discovered that he was the only person who saw and heard a certain car. The connection with cats became more pronounced when Lady Carmichael was found bathed in blood as if she had been attacked by a cat. Finally Arthur very nearly drowned after falling into a pond and remaining under water for nearly half an hour, only surfacing upon hearing the voice of his fiancée Phyllis Patterson.

(126)   1933

THE CALL OF WINGS

This story is concerned with Silas Hamer, a very rich man, and a self confessed materialist.

After a dinner given by the nerve specialist Bernard Seldon at which a parson from the East End of London, Richard Borrow was present, Harmer chooses to walk home. Whilst walking he sees a man run over by a bus but does nothing to try and save him. As he continues his walk he finds himself attracted by a flute player's music and begins to hallucinate. He imagines himself being carried upwards and his whole materialistic attitude is transformed.

Hamer gives all his money to the priest Richard Borrow and dies while he is trying to save someone who has thrown himself under a tube train.

(127)   1933

THE LAST SÉANCE

Simone who is engaged to Raoul Daubreuil is a medium who conducts séances with considerable success. However, she is anxious to give it up and her fiancée agrees providing she conducts one last séance for Madame Exe.

Simone agrees, however, this last séance is to have fatal consequences. Madame Exe who is anxious to contact her dead daughter Amelie, binds Raoul's hands and feet. Then when he is unable to help Simone, Madame Exe touches her dead daughter Amelie and Simone shrivels and dies.

(128)   1933

SOS

Mr. and Mrs. Dinsmead, their two daughters Magdalen and Charlotte, and their son Johnnie live in a house in Wiltshire far removed from the outside world. When Mortimer Cleveland has trouble with his car he finds it necessary to take shelter with the Dinsmeads. Upon entering the house, Mr. Cleveland who is an authority on mental science senses an air of tension. His suspicions are further aroused when he finds written in the dust on a table in his room the letters SOS. It is this appeal for help which stimulates him to try and find the reason for it.

(129)   1933

157

In an attempt to impress her friend Jim Masterton, Barbara St. Vincent, a woman of relatively impoverished circumstances rents a house in Westminster with a nominal rent and optional servants.

Mrs. St. Vincent moves into No. 7 Cheviott Place with her two children, Barbara and Rupert and acquires the services of the butler Quentin. However, Rupert's suspicions are aroused as he discovers that the house belonged to Lord Listerdale who disappeared to East Africa and left his power of attorney with one Colonel Maurice Carfox. One day whilst in King's Cheviott, Rupert sees another man like Quentin and brings him back to Cheviott Place. During the resulting confrontation it transpires that the St. Vincent's butler is Lord Listerdale and that the man Rupert found was the original butler.

Eventually all is resolved and Lord Listerdale and Mrs. St. Vincent fall in love.

(130)   1934

PHILOMEL COTTAGE

Miss Alix King and Dicky Windyford are very good friends, however, when Alix receives a legacy of £2000 she meets and marries Gerald Martin, and together they move into the isolated Philomel Cottage.

However, after some time Alix begins to feel uneasy about her new marriage. Her suspicions are fuelled by a talk she has with the gardener George and a diary she finds which belongs to Gerald. Finally Alix discovers some old American newspapers which mention the trial of a swindler and bigamist named Charles Lemaitre. Alix realises that Gerald is Charles Lemaitre and in her anxiety and fear for her life phones Dick Windyford for help.

(131)   1934

After having been fired by his uncle for not being serious enough, George Rowland decides to take a train to Rowland's Castle. While at Waterloo Station he meets a girl called Elizabeth who asks him to hide her from her uncle. When she leaves the train at Woking, Elizabeth tells George that he must follow one of the passengers at all costs, and anxious to make his journey more exciting points out arbitrarily a man with a black beard.

George dutifully follows the appointed man until he meets Detective Inspector Jarrold in Portsmouth. At this meeting it transpires that the man George has been following is a spy called Mardenberg. He also discovers that Elizabeth has been trying to avoid marrying her cousin Prince Karl, whom her uncle would like her to marry, by disguising herself as Grand Duchess Alexa of Catoria – her brother's proposed fiancée. However, the situation is finally resolved, when Elizabeth and George decide to get married.

(132)   1934

SING A SONG OF SIXPENCE

This story revolves around an investigation of the murder of Miss Lily Crabtree. Miss Crabtree of 18 Palatine Walk, Chelsea is found dead after being hit over the head, and, of the five occupants of her house, four are considered possible suspects. Martha, the household servant is considered above suspicion.

The four suspects are the twins, Magdalen and Matthew Vaughan, and Mr. and Mrs. Crabtree. In an attempt to solve the case Magdalen appeals to the retired barrister Sir Edward Pallister K.C. for help.

By questioning the individual members of the household Sir Edward is able to deduce who the murderer is. The most helpful piece of information which he receives is given to him by Martha who tells him how Lily was upset by getting a new sixpence back.

(133)   1934

THE MANHOOD OF
EDWARD ROBINSON

Edward Robinson is engaged to be married to a woman named Maud. However, at times, he becomes discontented and although he recognises that Maud is a sensible woman he often wishes that she had more faults and less virtues.

It is this dissatisfaction and his own desire for adventure which prevent him from telling Maud when he wins £500 in a competition. Believing that Maud would persuade him to save the money, Edward buys a car and goes away for a few days on his own. During this time he experiences a great deal of excitement when his car is mistakenly exchanged for a car belonging to Jimmy Folliot which contains a diamond necklace and a note.

As a result of this adventure, when Edward returns to Maud he feels that he is really a man.

(134)   1934

ACCIDENT

During a visit to his friend Captain Haydock, Evans, an ex-C.I.D. Inspector is introduced to Haydock's neighbours, Mr. and Mrs. Merrowdene. Evans recognises Mrs. Merrowdene as a woman named Mrs. Anthony who was suspected of murdering her husband after he had taken out a large life insurance policy for her benefit. Evans recalls that she was acquitted of this crime, but when he learns that Mr. Merrowdene has recently taken out a large life insurance policy he becomes concerned.

In an attempt to let Mrs. Merrowdene know that he suspects what she is going to do, Evans accepts an invitation to have tea with her. However, Evans proves unable to help Mr. Merrowdene, because Mrs. Merrowdene poisons him.

(135)   1934

JANE IN SEARCH OF A JOB

Jane Cleveland, who is out of a job is offered £3000 to impersonate the Grand Duchess Pauline of Ostrora at several public engagements. The Duchess fears that she may be kidnapped and is therefore unwilling to make any public appearances herself.

Jane accepts the job and during the official opening of a bazaar arrives as the journalist Miss Montressor and then goes into an outer room to change clothes. However, when Jane leaves the bazaar in her disguise as the Duchess she is kidnapped and drugged. When she finally wakes up she finds herself dressed as Miss Montressor once more.

In an attempt to discover the truth Jane tells her story to a young man who had followed her, and finally has the mystery explained to her by Detective Inspector Farrell.

(136)   1934

A FRUITFUL SUNDAY

Whilst driving in the country Miss Dorothy Pratt and Mr. Edward Palgrove stop at a fruit sellers to buy a basket of cherries. While eating the cherries by a river bank, they read in a Sunday paper about the theft of a necklace worth £50,000, and to their surprise they find in their basket a necklace fitting the description of the one which was stolen.

Neither of them can decide whether or not to keep the necklace until Ted makes a discovery which solves their dilemma for them.

(137)   1934

MR. EASTWOOD'S ADVENTURE

Mr. Anthony Eastwood is just settling down to begin writing his novel entitled, "The Mystery of the Second Cucumber", when he is interrupted by a telephone call from a woman named Carmen asking for help. When he arrives at 320 Kirk Street, he is mistaken for Conrad Fleckman and arrested by the police for the murder of Anna Rosenberg.

Anthony Eastwood returns to his own home with the two policeman who arrested him, and while he has a drink with the Inspector, the sergeant called Carter searches the house. To pass the time the Inspector tells Eastwood about the murder they are investigating and the tale of the shawl of the Thousand Flowers.

Remark   Alternative title
The Mystery of the Spanish Shawl

(138)   1934

THE GOLDEN BALL

While walking through London after being fired by his wealthy uncle Ephraim Leadbetter, George Durdas is invited by Mary Montressor to step into her car. Mary, who is engaged to the Duke of Edgehill then asks George if he would like to marry her.

The situation escalates, and George soon finds himself looking for a house in the country with Mary. When they find a house they like they discover that it is occupied by a couple called Pardonstenger, and that Mr. Pardonstenger has no intention of selling them the house. Instead he forces them to go upstairs where he plans to lock them in a room. However, George has the presence of mind to kick Mr. Pardonstenger downstairs and he and Mary manage to escape.

(139)   1934

THE RAJAH'S EMERALD

While staying in Kimpton-on-Sea, James Bond uses a bathing-hut belonging to Lord Campion. After bathing he goes to lunch and while he is eating discovers that he has an emerald in the pocket of his trousers. The situation becomes more complicated when he reads in a newspaper that another guest of Lord Campion's, the Rajah of Maraputna has had an emerald stolen. James deduces that he must have put the wrong pair of trousers on after bathing.

When Detective Inspector Merrilees tries to get the emerald from James he refuses to hand it over and instead insists upon taking the Detective Inspector to the police station.

(140)   1934

SWAN SONG

While in London the famous operatic star Madame Paula Nazorkoff is asked by Lady Rustonbury to sing "Tosca" at Rustonbury Castle. Madame Nazorkoff and her manager Mr. Cowan agree, and it is arranged that Signor Roscari will play Scarpiz.

However, a few hours before the concert Signor Roscari is taken ill and is unable to perform. Fortunately Edward Bréon, a retired French baritone who lives nearby agrees to take his place, but during the performance he is stabbed to death.

(141)   1934

169

THE CASE OF THE MIDDLE-AGED WIFE

After reading an advertisement in the morning paper advocating that unhappy people should consult Mr Parker Pyne of 17 Richmond Street, Mrs Maria Packington does so. She is unhappy because her husband George has a girlfriend, and it is in an attempt to remedy this unhappiness that she goes to visit Mr Parker Pyne.

After paying a 200 guinea advance, Maria visits a beauty specialist, a dress maker and a hairdressers and begins to go out to lunches, dinners and dancing with an attractive young man called Claude Luttrel. On one particular evening when Maria is at a night club with Claude they meet George with his girlfriend, and George's interest in his wife is rekindled.

(142)   1934

THE CASE OF THE DISCONTENTED SOLDIER

On his retirement from an army posting in East Africa, Major Wilbrahams finds that he is both unhappy and bored. He consults Mr. Parker Pyne, one of whose staff, Miss Madeleine de Sara, discovers the Major's preference in women.

Meanwhile Miss Freda Clegg has also consulted Mr. Parker Pyne, and it appears that she may well be the sort of woman with whom Major Wilbrahams could have an affinity. Both the Major and Miss Clegg receive written invitations to different houses in Hampstead which, significantly are both in Friar's Lane.

However, before the Major reaches his destination on the date in question, he becomes involved in rescuing Miss Clegg from two assailants.

Thereafter the Major and Miss Clegg enjoy a number of exciting experiences together and strike up a relationship which culminates in marriage.

(143)   1934

THE CASE OF THE DISTRESSED LADY

Mr. Parker Pyne receives a visit from Mrs. Daphne St. John, who explains that she has stolen a platinum ring from Lady Dortheimer by exchanging the real ring for a paste replica. Now she wishes to make amends by returning the stolen ring, but being unsure as to how this can be achieved, she enlists Mr. Parker Pyne's aid.

Mr. Parker Pyne does indeed help, but not in the manner which Mrs. St. John has envisaged. With the assistance of two of his staff members, Claude Luttrel and Madeleine de Sara, Mr Pyne discovers that the so-called 'stolen' ring is in fact a paste replica.

(144)   1934

THE CASE OF THE DISCONTENTED HUSBAND

After nine years of marriage, Mrs. Iris Wade is bored by her husband and becomes involved with another man called Sinclair Jordan.

Mr. Reginald Wade is understandably unhappy and, on seeing one of Mr. Parker Pyne's advertisements, decides to make an appointment with him. As a result, it is decided that one of Mr. Pyne's staff, Miss Madeleine de Sara should act as Reggies's girlfriend in the hope of making Iris jealous.

The plot does indeed work, for Iris wants Reggie back. There is, however, a problem to be solved before husband and wife can be brought back together again . . . . for Reginald has fallen in love with his conspirator Madeleine.

(145)   1934

Mr. Roberts is a hardworking man who is careful with his money, but, when his wife and children go off to stay at his mother-in-law's home, Mr. Roberts enquires if Mr. Parker Pyne can suggest something that will offer him a break from his usual routine for a short period.

Mr. Pyne has a solution, for, knowing that his friend, Mr. Bonnington, is anxious to have certain papers dispatched to Geneva, he proposes that Roberts should act as a courier.

Roberts makes a good job of his task and receives fifty pounds for his trouble.

(146)   1934

THE CASE OF THE RICH WOMAN

Mrs. Amelia Rymer has been a wealthy widow for five years, but despite having everything that she needs, she is still unhappy, and so arranges a consultation with Mr. Parker Pyne.

A week later when a number of preparations have been completed, Mrs. Rymer is drugged when introduced to 'Eastern Magic' by a Doctor Constantine.

On awaking, she finds that she is no longer the wealthy Mrs. Rymer, but simply Hannah Moorhouse, a farmhouse helper and expected to work in the same way she did before she became rich.

Although at first she is angry with Mr. Pyne, eventually she does indeed find happiness, as well as a new husband, Joe Welsh, a farm-hand. After setting aside a certain sum of money for the purchase of a farm, Amelia donates the rest of her considerable wealth to charity.

(147)   1934

HAVE YOU GOT EVERYTHING YOU WANT?

Travelling with the Simplon from Paris to Istanboul, Mr. Parker Pyne meets Mrs. Elsie Jeffries on the train. She tells him that while still at home, she had been able to make out just a few lines on a ink blotter: 'wife . . . . Simplon Express . . . . just before Venice would be the best time'·

Just before the Express reaches Venice, a fire breaks out, the result, it seems of a smoke bomb. After all the fuss has died down, Mrs. Jeffries discovers that her jewels are missing. But when one suspect, Madame Subayska, who had the opportunity to steal them is searched, nothing is found.

On arrival in Trieste, Mr. Parker Pyne sends off a cable to Mr. Jeffries who is in Istanboul; and when the Simplon Express reaches its destination, Mr. Parker Pyne meets up with Edward Jeffries.

(148)   1934

176

THE GATE OF BAGHDAD

A number of people are travelling from Damascus to Baghdad: the party includes Mr. Parker Pyne, Miss Pryce and her niece Netta, Mr Hensley, Captain Smethurst, Mrs Pentemian and her son, General Poli.

The party also includes three airforce officers, Mr. O'Rourke, Mr. Williamson and Mr. Loftus who is also a doctor.

At one of their stopping places, Captain Smethurst is found dead. By careful investigation and logical reasoning, Mr Parker Pyne ascertains that the unfortunate man has been murdered and also that one of the group is responsible for the Captain's death.

(149)   1934

When flying from Baghdad to Shiraz in Persia, Mr. Parker Pyne hears a tale from his German pilot, Herr Schlagal.

The pilot explains how some years previously he had been responsible for flying Lady Esther Carr and her companion, Muriel King, to the same destination that Pyne was making for now.

Herr Schlagal fell in love with Muriel King, but unfortunately Lady Esther became infatuated with Herr Schlagal.

Shortly after their flight, Muriel was to fall from her balcony to her death.

Mr. Parker Pyne is acquainted with Lord and Lady Icheldever, Lady Esther's parents, and is aware that they both have blue eyes. However he hears from the British consul that their daughter, Lady Esther has dark eyes . . . . . a fact which leads Parker Pyne to the conclusion that some deception has taken place.

(150)   1934

THE PEARL OF PRICE

Travelling from Amman to the camp in Petra is a party of tourists which includes the American magnate, Mr. Caleb P. Blundell, his daughter Carol, his secretary Jim Hurst, Sir Donald Marvel M.P., the archaeologist Dr. Carver and Colonel Dubosc as well as Mr. Parker Pyne and the guide Abbas Effendi.

Miss Blundell is wearing a pair of pearl earrings which, according to her Father, are worth 80,000 dollars.

When Carol loses one of the earrings Jim Hurst, known to once have been a thief, is a prime suspect.

(151)   1934

On the steam-ship Fayoum, sailing up the Nile from Assouan to Cairo, are passengers Sir George and Lady Ariadne Grayle, Sir George's niece Pamela Grayle, his secretary Basil West, as well as Lady Grayle's nurse Miss MacNaughton and Mr. Parker Pyne. Lady Grayle is very rich, and according to her nurse, unwell rather than really ill. One day Parker Pyne is consulted by Lady Grayle who suspects that her husband is trying to poison her. Miss MacNaughton is also concerned for her charge's safety.

When Lady Grayle does indeed die, Parker Pyne forces a confession from one of the passengers.

(152)   1934

Mr. Parker Pyne is travelling incognito under the name of Mr. Thompson. While staying in a hotel in Delphi, Greece, he learns that someone else, calling himself Parker Pyne is being consulted by Mrs. Willard J. Peters, who refers to him as 'the good gentleman'.

Mrs. Willard J. Peters has consulted him because her son Willard is being held captive, to be freed on the payment of a ransom: her diamond necklace.

The 'good gentleman' suggests that they replace the diamonds by paste stones, which he will then take to the kidnappers, allowing Mrs. Peters to ensure the saftey of the real diamonds.

(153)   1934

At number 14, Bardsley Gardens Mews, live Mrs. Barbara Allen, nee Armitage, and Miss Jane Plendenleith.

On the evening of the fifth of November, while Jane is away for a long weekend, Barbara, following a visit from Major Eustace, commits suicide.

The man in charge of the investigations is Chief Inspector Japp, who invites Hercule Poirot to come along.

The initial interrogations suggest that Barbara has been murdered, but Poirot is unconvinced.

(154)   1937

THE INCREDIBLE THEFT

The first Minister of Defence Lord Mayfield, who previously as Sir Charles McLaughlin was head of an engineering firm, has invited a number of people to join him for a weekend party.

They include Air Marshall Sir George Carrington, his wife Julia and their son Reggie; Mrs. Vanderlyn, who has contacts in three countries mostly with men with navy or airforce backgrounds, and a number of other guests.

When Sir George expresses some surprise at Mrs. Vanderlyn's inclusion in the guest list, Lord Mayfield explains that he wants to set a trap for her.

After dinner, Lord Mayfield and Sir George intend to discuss some important plans, but, on returning from a short stroll in the fresh air, they discover that the most important plans, the specifications of a new bomber, have disappeared.

Sir George enlists the aid of Monsieur Poirot.

(155)   1937

M. Hercule Poirot receives a letter from Gervase Chevenix-Gore requesting that Poirot be prepared to travel to Hamborough Close, Hamborough St. Mary, Westshire, and be ready to deal with a problem which requires some discretion.

Some days later, Poirot receives a telegram saying that he is expected .

However, when M. Poirot arrives it is to find that Gervase Chevenix-Gore has committed suicide in his study: and it appears that he has shot himself, the bullet rebounding off the mirror.

Hercule Poirot finds this particular suicide situation somewhat strange.

The Chief Constable, Major Riddle, and Poirot both question a number of people. They include the dead man's wife, Vanda and her daughter Ruth, a nephew Hugo Trent, a guest Susan Coldwell, as well as a friend of the family, Colonel Ned Bury, and the family lawyer Ogilvie Forbes.

Also interrogated are the late Gervase Chevenix Gore's secretary, Godfrey Burrows, the assistant Miss Lingard, Captain Lake the agent for the estate, and the butler Snell.

(156)   1937

TRIANGLE AT RHODES

M. Poirot is taking a holiday on the Island of Rhodes. After making the acquaintance of a group of guests he forsees the possibility of a murder resulting from an eternal triangle relationship.

Apart from Miss Pamela Ryall, Miss Susan Blake and General Barnes, there are also two couples in residence: Mr. Tony and Mrs. Valentine Chantry and Mr. Douglas Cameron who is with Mrs. Marjorie Emma Gold.

Marjorie appears to be a pleasant woman, but Douglas is attracted to Valentine, to her husband's obvious anger.

It appears to Pamela and Susan that the eternal triangle exists between Valentine, Tony and Douglas, and when Valentine dies after drinking a pink gin laced with stropanthin, Douglas is arrested.

(157)   1937

Mr. Isaac Pointa, a diamond merchant, has invited a number of guests to a private dinner in The Royal George, Dartmouth.

The guest list includes his partner Leon Stein, Sir George and Lady Pamela Marroway, Mr. Samuel Leathern, his daughter Eve, as well as Mrs. Jane Rushington and Mr. Evan Llewellyn.

During the dinner, Mr. Pointa at Eve's request, passes round the large Morning Star diamond. At a certain point, the stone is found to have disappeared, and efforts to trace it prove unsuccessful.

Suspicion falls on Mr. Llewellyn, chiefly because he is known to be the only person to have had any contact with the outside world during the evening.

Mr. Llewellyn consults Parker Pyne hoping that he will be able to prove his innocence.

(158)   1939

THE MYSTERY OF THE
BAGHDAD CHEST

Major Jack Rich has invited Mr. Edward and Mrs. Marguerita Clayton, Major Curtiss, and Mr. and Mrs. Spence to a party.

Edward Clayton, however, is called away to Scotland but before he leaves, he has a drink with Major Curtiss and calls on Major Rich in order to explain that he will be unable to join the party.

He finds that Major Rich is not at home, but the valet, Burgoyne, shows him into the sitting-room to wait. However, by the time the Major returns home, Clayton has already gone.

The next morning, Burgoyne discovers Clayton lying murdered in a chest: and Jack Rich is suspected of being his killer.

During a party at Lady Chatterton's house, Marguerita asks Hercule Poirot to prove Jack's innocence.

(159)   1939

HOW DOES YOUR GARDEN GROW?

M. Poirot receives a letter from a Miss Amelia Jane Barrowby, who lives with her niece Mrs. Mary Delafontaine at Roseband, Charman's Green, Buckinghamshire.

In her letter, Miss Barrowby requests M. Poirot to investigate a number of matters, but when he writes back to her, he receives no correspondence in return; and his secretary Miss Lemon indicates the reason . . . . . Miss Barrowby has died.

When Poirot pays a visit to Roseband, he meets Miss Barrowby's niece, as well as her husband and a Russian girl, Katrina who turns out to have been nurse-companion to the dead woman.

Hercule Poirot is convinced that Miss Barrowby has been murdered, but is puzzled as to the reason for death, and the identity of the culprit.

However, the post mortem reveals that Miss Barrowby has been the victim of strychnine poisoning; and when Miss Lemon discovers that Mary Delafontaine had bought a dozen and half oysters, M. Poirot's attention is attracted by some shells lying in the garden.

(160)   1939

PROBLEM AT POLLENSA BAY

Mr. Parker Pyne is on holiday, staying at the Hotel Pino d'Oro, Pollensa Bay, Majorca.

The other hotel guests include Mrs. R. Adela Chester and her son, Basil. Mr. Parker Pyne believes Mrs. Chester to be unhappy but is reluctant to either offer his help, or to tell her of his profession.

A Mrs. Vina Wycherley of the Hotel Mariposa discloses Parker Pyne's identity and Amelia Chester turns to him for help.

Apparently, Basil is engaged to someone called Betty Gregg, of whom Mrs. Chester disapproves. Christopher Parker Pyne asks for Maggie Sayer's help with the problem.

He persuades Basil to take out Maggie who pretends to be 'Dolores Ramona', who Basil's mother is likely to dislike even more. In the end, Adela Chester comes to like Betty, and after two weeks approves the engagement of the happy couple.

(161)   1939

YELLOW IRIS

While living in a Spanish-speaking country, M. Poirot is telephoned one evening by a woman who asks him to come to a certain restaurant, and tells him to look out for the table with the yellow irises on it.

Poirot goes to the Jardin des Cynes Restaurant and at the correct table he meets Anthony Chapell, who explains that the reservation has been made by Mr. Barton Russell, and that they are to be joined by a number of other guests, to include Pauline Weatherby, Russell's sister-in-law, Serona Lola Valdez, and Stephen Carter of the Diplomatic Service.

The host, Barton Russell tells his guests and M. Poirot, that the dinner is being held in memory of his late wife, Iris, who had died some four years previously while attending a dinner with the same people. The official version is that she died as a result of self-administered potassium cyanide.

(162)   1939

Miss Jane Marple tells her nephew, Raymond and his wife Joan, a story in which she has played a vital part.

Mr. Rhodes and his wife Amy are staying at the Crown Hotel, Banchester which is some twenty miles from St. Mary Mead.

One night Mrs. Rhodes is asleep in the bedroom, and her husband is working in the adjoining room, leaving the connecting door open. When, at eleven o'clock, Mr. Rhodes takes a book into the bedroom, he finds that his wife, Amy has been killed . . . . . stabbed with a stiletto dagger.

The only person who had entered the bedroom was the chamber-maid, but suspicion falls on the dead woman's husband who consults Miss Marple.

Miss Marple suspects that one of two women staying at the hotel is responsible.

(163)   1939

THE DREAM

Mr. Benedict Farley, a very wealthy man who lives in the Northway House requests M. Poirot to pay him a visit.

During the appointment, which is conducted in his secretary Hugo Cornworthy's room, Farley explains that every night for some time he has had a recurring dream in which, at 15.28, he shoots himself.

Hercule Poirot is unable to shed much light on the problem and takes his leave. A week later, however, Farley's doctor John Stillingfleet calls Poirot back to the house, explaining that his patient appears to have killed himself at approximately 15.28.

A number of important questions are raised, however. Why was Poirot involved at all?

Why should it be that Farley, who was wearing his glasses, still did not read the note which Poirot handed to him?

Poirot however, finds the solution.

(164)   1939

IN A GLASS DARKLY

Mr. X, who is a friend of Neil Carslake is spending a few days at the Carslake home in Badgeworthy.

While dressing, Mr. X glances in the mirror and sees a girl being strangled by a man but when he turns round, he finds there is no door through to the next room.

Later, he is introduced to Neil's sister, Sylvia and her fiance, Charles Crawley, and he recognises them as the couple he has seen in the mirror.

On leaving Badgeworthy, Mr. X tells his story to Sylvia who then breaks off her engagement.

After the War, Sylvia explains to Mr. X that her reason for breaking off her engagement was that she had fallen in love with Mr. X. The couple are then married; but the new husband is extremely jealous, to the point of almost strangling Sylvia, one day. Happily, however, he stops himself in time and the experience so shocks him, his jealousy is ended forever.

(165)   1939

PROBLEM AT SEA

A group of people on a sea voyage to Alexandria include Mrs. Adeline Clapperton, formerly the late Lord Carrington's wife who later married the music hall entertainer, Colonel John Clapperton.

Also present are General Forbes, Hercule Poirot, Miss Ellie Henderson, Kitty Mooney and Pam Cregan. Colonel Clapperton is henpecked by his wife who holds the purse-strings.

Mrs. Clapperton is found dead in her cabin, which has apparently been locked from the inside. She has been stabbed with a dagger; and several people are said to have overheard her talking through the locked door to her husband, John, prior to his going ashore.

When asked for his help by Ellie and the Captain, Hercule Poirot has an idea which is later proved to be correct.

Remark   Alternative title
                Murder at Sea

(166)   1939

THE NEMEAN LION

Lady Milly Hoggin's Pekinese dog, Shan Tung, is stolen, but is returned unharmed on payment of £200 ransom.

When Sir Joseph Hoggin learns of the affair, and that his friend Jacob Samuelson's wife has suffered a similiar experience, he asks M. Poirot to conduct an investigation and to put an end to such criminal activities.

Poirot's enquiries reveal that Lady Hoggin's companion, Miss Amy Carnaby also has a Pekinese dog, whose name it appears is Augustus; and apparently, Miss Carnaby has formed an association with a number of ladies companions who are also poorly paid.

Poirot ascertains that each time one of the group had to walk her mistress's dog, the Pekinese would be stolen and its place taken by Augustus. The replacement's lead would be cut during the walk, leaving Augustus to return of his own accord to the house which Amy occupied with her invalid sister-in-law.

Poirot retrieves the money for his client and receives the money back in payment of his fee, which he in turn donates to Amy's fund, knowing that the dog-napping crimes will now cease.

(167)   1947

THE LERNEAN HYDRA

Since the death, one year previously, of the wife of Dr. Charles Oldfeld, of Market Loughborough, a number of disturbing rumours have been circulating.

They hint that the Doctor, intending to marry his dispenser, Jean Moncrieffe, has disposed of his own wife. Somewhat concerned, the Doctor asks for Hercule Poirot's assistance in this matter.

Poirot first pays a visit to the worst slanderer, Miss Leatheran, and then sees the late Mrs. Oldfield's attendant, Nurse Harrison. Although the latter initially dislikes the suggestion, she later agrees to a post mortem being conducted on her patient.

This reveals that Mrs. Oldfield has indeed been killed.

(168)   1947

THE ARCADIAN DEER

M. Hercule Poirot's car breaks down in the village of Hartley Dene.

It was in this particular village, some months previously, that Ted Williamson from the garage had met the dancer Mademoiselle Katrina Samoushenka's young maid, Nita. Since Nita left, Ted has been unable to contact her and so he enlists Poirot's aid. When investigations are made, it seems that Mademoiselle was so taken with Ted, that one afternoon, the dancer disguised herself as her own lady's maid.

It is Poirot's opinion that Mademoiselle Samoushenka will indeed go back to Ted.

(169)   1947

THE ERYMANTHIAN BOAR

Hercule Poirot takes the funicular railway from Aldermatt, Switzerland, to Les Avines and while he is on the train, the conductor hands him a wad of paper. It is a letter from his old friend Lementeuil, the Swiss Commissioner of Police.

The Commissioner requests that Poirot takes the train all the way up to the Hotel Rocher Neiges, where Inspector Drouet is already staying, and where the known killer, Marrascuad, intends meeting up with a number of other people.

Other hotel guests include Dr. Karl Lutz from Vienna, Mr. Schwarz an American, Madame Grandier . . . and three rough-looking men.

Gustave, the waiter, introduces himself as Inspector Drouet, explaining that the previous waiter, Robert has left.

(170)   1947

THE AUGEAN STABLES

Edward Ferrier, the Prime Minister is the son-in-law of the previous man to hold such an office, John Hammett.

Hammett is accused by the editor of the X-Ray News, Percy Perry, of having misused party funds to his own advantage.

Believing John to be a crook, and the accusations to have some foundation, Edward fears for the political consequences of such revelations, and turns to Hercule Poirot for advice, hoping that the affair of the Augean Stables can be solved.

With the help of a friend, and Miss Thelma Anderson, who happens to bear a strong resemblance to Ferrier's wife, Poirot sees to it that the X-Ray News publishes scandalous pictures and stories about the Prime Minister's wife.

The X-Ray News is found guilty of misconduct, and as a consequence the accusations levelled at the ex-Prime Minister, John Hammett will remain either unpublished . . . or not be believed.

(171)   1947

THE STYMPHALEAN BIRDS

The politician, Harold Waring is taking a vacation in a hotel in Herzoslovakia, where he meets a Mrs. Rice and her daughter, Mrs. Elsie Clayton.

Mrs. Clayton's husband Philip (who according to the two women, is a brute) has remained behind in England.

Philip Clayton, however, contrary to expectations has arrived at the hotel and, after a fight, dies as a result from a blow from a paper-weight thrown at him by his wife.

Concerned for Elsie, Harold Waring advances her the money with which to bribe the local police and the hotel staff.

(172)   1947

Miss Diana Maberly consults Hercule Poirot and explains to him that her fiance has broken off their engagement, and that she needs Poirot's help.

Miss Maberly's fiance, Hugh Chandler is the son of Admiral Sir Charles Chandler, whose wife Caroline had drowned some years ago.

Hugh, it seems, has broken off the engagement, believing himself to be insane.

However, Hercule Poirot is able to prove that Hugh Chandler is not mad, but being poisoned with datura.

(173)   1947

THE HORSES OF DIOMEDES

Hercule Poirot receives a call from his friend Dr. Michael Stoddart, who asks him to come to the home of a certain Mrs Grace, where a party involving the use of cocaine has taken place.

Dr. Stoddart is in attendance in his professional capacity, but he is also acquainted with one of the guests, Sheila Grant, who is one of General Grant's four daughters.

M. Poirot is interested in uncovering the source of the cocaine operation as one of Sheila's friends, Anthony Hawker is a suspect.

(174)   1947

THE GIRDLE OF HYPPOLITA

A Rubens painting has been stolen from Simpson's Gallery and suspecting that a certain French millionaire is responsible, Alexander Simpson asks Poirot to see if he can get the canvas back.

Meanwhile, Inspector Japp has also asked Poirot to cooperate with him in the case of the kidnapped schoolgirl, Winnie King.

Winnie, on her way to a school for young ladies in Neuilly has disappeared just outside Amiens, leaving a hat and a pair of shoes by the side of a railway line.

The next day, Winnie turns up. She has been doped and left by the side of the road outside Amiens.

Poirot is interested to learn just how, and indeed what the motive for the kidnapping has been. And of course, he discovers the truth.

(175)   1947

THE FLOCK OF GERYON

A religious sect named the Flock of the Shepherd has been established by a certain Dr. Andersen, who calls himself The Great Shepherd.

One of the members dies, leaving a will bequeathing all her property to the sect. Her name was Emmeline Clegg, a friend of Amy Carnaby who is an acquaintance of Hercule Poirot.

It appears that three members of the sect, all lonely women have already died, and Amy suspects that her friend's death is the result of foul play. She suggests to Poirot that she assists him in his enquiries.

(176)   1947

THE APPLES OF THE HESPERIDES

The great art collector, Emery Power has bought the Borgia goblet, which bears the apple-tree and serpent design, from the Marchese di San Veratrino.

Before the goblet can be despatched to its new owner, it is stolen, almost certainly by Dublay, Riccovetti and Patrick Casey.

The first two are arrested, but the goblet's whereabouts remains a mystery.

Some ten years later, Emery Power, who is convinced that Reuben Rosenthal is in possession of the goblet, receives information to the contrary. He therefore enlists the aid of Hercule Poirot, who is somewhat surprised by the fact that there has been no word about the goblet at all, in such a long time.

(177)   1947

THE CAPTURE OF CERBERUS

After a gap of some twenty years, Poirot encounters the Countess Vera Rossakoff at Piccadilly Circus, but there is only time for her to blurt, "You can find me in Hell".

Hercule Poirot's secretary, Miss Lemon, explains to him that 'Hell' is in fact a night club which is run by a Russian woman.

Poirot pays the club a visit and learns that it is owned by a known criminal, Paul Varesco. Poirot is also introduced to Dr. Alice Cunningham, who, it seems, is a psychologist.

(178)   1947

THE SECOND GONG

Mr. Hubert Pytcham Roche is a somewhat eccentric man. Each day, at his home, the dinner gong is first sounded at 08.05, and repeated at 8.15, with any late-comers never being asked for dinner again.

One particular day, dinner is postponed by Mr. Lytcham Roche for a few minutes, the reason being that the train is late. However, the first gong is presumed by Joan Ashby, one of the guests, to be the second.

Some minutes later, a shot rings out.

On the late train is Hercule Poirot, who has been asked by Lytcham Roche to investigate a financial matter. When he breaks open the study door, he finds his host lying dead.

The dead man appears to have shot himself, for the weapon is lying beside him and all the doors and windows are firmly closed.

However, enquiries reveal otherwise.

(179)   1948

Mrs. Lyon of 74, Culver Street is found strangled.

In their guest house, Monkswell Manor, Giles and Molly Davis are expecting their first guests, Mrs. Boyle, Major Metcalf, Mr. Wren and an unexpected guest called Mr. Paravincini.

Inspector Parminter has reason to believe that the next scene of a murder might well be Monkswell Manor.

The Manor is completely snowed up, and after Detective Sergeant Trotter arrives, even the telephone is cut off. At a certain point, Trotter relates the tale of three evacuee children who were billeted in 1940 at Longridge Farm, which was the property of John and Maureen Gregg.

The Greggs were found guilty and sentenced to prison terms for the criminal neglect of one of the children. John Gregg escaped from prison, and later died. His wife was released from custody two months previously, taking the precaution to change her name to Mrs. Lyon, the name of the woman found strangled.

One of the guest house residents, is also found strangled, and it is revealed that they had been the billeting officer in charge of the evacuee arrangements.

(180)   1950

STRANGE JEST

Charmian Stroud and Edward Rossiter are desperate.

Their Uncle Mathew, whom they believed to be a wealthy man, has died and left everything to his niece and nephew, who however, are unable to locate the money.

Their friend, Jane Hellier, introduces them to Miss Marple who during the course of her investigations discovers a secret drawer in the dead man's desk.

Lying in the drawer is a cookery recipe for baked lamb, and also a number of love letters sent from all over the world from a certain Betty Martin.

They are part of a code.

(181)   1950

TAPE-MEASURE MURDER

Miss Politt, a dressmaker in St. Mary Mead, has an appointment with Mrs. Spenlow, who, however, fails to answer Miss Politt's knock.

Mrs. Spenlow is found dead.

When Miss Marple investigates, she discovers that Miss Politt had, in fact, been in the house of her client prior to knocking on the front door.

(182)   1950

THE CASE OF THE PERFECT MAID

The Old Hall, St. Mary Mead, has been divided up into four flats.

In one of the flats live Lavinia and Emily Skinner, the latter always being unwell. When the Skinner women's maid is accused of stealing, she is sacked immediately, and a new maid engaged.

However, the new maid disappears one day, along with the valuables of all the residents of the Old Hall.

Miss Marple, who has her suspicions about the new maid, Mary Higgings, has found a number of finger-prints, and she suggests to the inspector in charge of the case that it might be useful to check them with others in the Old Hall.

(183)   1950

THE CASE OF THE CARETAKER

Miss Marple has the 'flu, and to give her something to think about, Dr. Haydock leaves her a manuscript to study while she is confined to bed. The manuscript holds certain information, which proves to be interesting.

Harry and Louise Laxton live in Kingdean House, which is in a village. One day, while out riding, Louise's horse is startled when the caretaker's wife, Mrs. Murgatroyd calls out. When the horse throws his rider she is killed.

Miss Marple makes certain enquiries and comes to the conclusions which Dr. Haydock confirms, and it seems that Dr. Haydock has also given Miss Marple the right prescription for her own illness!

(184)   1950

THE THIRD FLOOR FLAT

Patricia Garnett lives on the fourth floor in a flat in Friar Mansions, London.

One evening, she arrives at her front door in the company of her friends, Mildred Hope, Jimmy Faulkener and Donovan Bailey, but she is unable to find her key.

Jimmy and Donovan decide to get upstairs by the coal-lift, but by mistake arrive on the third floor at Mrs. Ernestine Grant's flat.

The occupant is dead.

The police are called to the scene of the crime, but they are also joined by a certain Mr. O'Connor who lives on the floor above Patricia Garnett, and who is in fact Poirot, incognito.

Poirot solves the case.

(185)   1950

THE ADVENTURE OF
JOHNNIE WAVERLY

Mr. and Mrs. Waverly of Waverly Court, Surrey, have enlisted M. Poirot's aid.

Their three year old son, Johnnie, has been kidnapped, and they have received a ransom demand for £50,000.

The boy's mother is a wealthy woman, but Waverly, who enjoys the good life, is kept rather short of funds by his wife, who holds the purse strings.

(186)   1950

FOUR AND TWENTY
BLACKBIRDS

While Henry Bonnington and Hercule Poirot are having dinner at the Gallant Endeavour, the waitress, Molly, tells them about a special guest.

He has been nicknamed 'Old Father Time', and for ten years he has taken dinner on Tuesdays and Thursdays.

The previous week, however, 'Old Father Time' had come in on Monday, and had ordered a meal quite different from his usual taste.

Hercule Poirot becomes curious and his enquiries reveal that the regular guest, who is in fact Henry Gascoigne, passed away only a matter of hours after his wealthy twin brother, Anthony died from natural causes.

(187)   1950

While spending an evening in London with Mr. Satterthwaite, Colonel Melrose, the Chief Constable is recalled to his home.

Inspector Curtis informs his senior officer that Sir James Duighton has been murdered at Alderway, his estate. Satterthwaite accompanies the Colonel to the dead man's estate, and on their way they meet Mr. Harley Quin who is also making for the same place.

Investigations reveal that Sir James has been the victim of a blow to the head, but Lady Laura insists that she has shot him, while Paul Delangua, her friend, asserts that he is responsible for stabbing Sir James.

The Chief Constable and the others think that Laura and Paul are innocent.

(188)   1950

THE UNDERDOG

When Sir Reuben Astwell is found murdered in the Tower Room at his home, Mon Repos in Abbot's Cross, his nephew, Charles Leverson is arrested.

However, Lady Nancy Aswell is convinced that it is really the dead man's secretary, Owen Trefusis who is guilty.

She therefore asks for Hercule Poirot's help, through her own secretary, Lily Margrave. The detective's enquiries reveal that Sir Reuben had double-crossed Lily's brother Humphrey Naylor, in the matter of the Mpala Gold Fields. When Naylor turns out to be staying in Abbot's Cross, he and his sister Lily are certainly possible suspects.

However, Lady Astwell stood, along with Charles, to inherit Sir Reuben's money.

(189)   1950

The 12.14 train from Paddington to Plymouth stops at Bristol, Weston-Super-Mare, Taunton, Exeter and Newton Abbott.

Lieutenant Alec Simpson, R.N., boards the train at Newton Abbott and finds a woman's body lying under the seat. She has been stabbed, and it appears that the dead woman is Mrs. Rupert Carrington, the daughter of the U.S. steel magnate, Ebeneezer Halliday.

Mrs. Carrington had reserved a seat as far as Bristol, and it had been arranged that her maid, Jane Mason should travel in the next carriage. According to Jane, Mrs. Carrington had told her that she was to alight, with the luggage at Bristol, and to wait there for her mistress who was travelling some distance further.

The dead woman's father, Ebeneezer Halliday, turns to Hercule Poirot to solve the mystery of his daughter's stabbing and while Inspector Japp discovers the murder weapon lying somewhere between Weston and Taunton, M. Poirot uses his quick wits to solve the crime.

(190)   1951

THE AFFAIR AT THE
VICTORY BALL

The fifth Viscount, Lord Cronshaw accompanies his friends, Miss Coco Courtenay, the Honourable Eustace Beltane, his uncle, Mrs. Mallaby, and Mr. and Mrs. Chris Davidson to the Victory Ball being held in the Colossus Hall, London. The party go dressed as the commedia dell'arte characters, Harlequin, Columbine, Punchinello, Pulcinella, Pierrot and Pierette. Miss Coco leaves the ball early, and later dies from an accidental overdose of cocaine. Curiously, Lord Cronshaw is found murdered in the Hall. When he is asked by Inspector Japp to be of some assistance, Poirot discovers that Chris Davidson, who had seen Miss Coco home, had arrived at the ball dressed as Harlequin, but later changed into Pierrot's costume.

(191)   1951

Inspector Japp, Poirot and Captain Hastings are spending a weekend in the country at Market Basing, when Constable Pollard asks for the Inspector's advice. It would appear, the Constable explain's, that Mr. Walter Protheroe of Leigh House, has either been murdered or has shot himself. According to Dr. Giles, suicide can be ruled out, for the bullet entered the victim's head behind the left ear, and the pistol was found in the right hand. Hercule Poirot notices that although the windows are closed and the ash-tray full of cigarette stubs, remarkably, the air is fresh. Also,. the dead man's hankerchief is in his right sleeve.

Despite the circumstantial evidence then, investigations reveal that Walter Protheroe has indeed killed himself; and his house-keeper, Mrs. Clegg, had been responsible for closing the window, and changing the pistol over from his left to his right hand. Enquiries indicate that the dead man had been the victim of a blackmailer, a certain Mr. Parker, who knew that Protheroe's real name was Wendover, and that in 1910 he had been involved in the explosion of a cruiser.

(192)   1951

THE LEMESURIER INHERITANCE

A curse has been placed on the Lemesurier family
to the effect that no first-born son shall inherit.
While Hercule Poirot and Captain Hastings are
having a conversation with Captain Vincent
Lemesurier at the Carlton in London, Lemesurier
receives the news that his father has been killed in
an accident. However, the next day, Poirot learns
from a newspaper report that the Captain is also
dead, having, it seems, thrown himself out of a
train. On Vincent's death, the new heir becomes his
Uncle Ronald who only survives two years before
being succeeded by another Uncle, named John.
However, not only does John's son commit
suicide, but John himself dies from the effect of a
wasp bite, the Lemesurier Inheritance passing
thereafter to the late Captain Vincent's uncle,
Hugo, who is the father of two sons, Ronald and
Gerald. After the first son, Ronald, has survived
three narrow escapes from death, his mother turns
to Poirot for help.

(193)   1951

Hercule Poirot and Captain Hastings receive a visit from Mrs. Pengelly from Polgarwith in Cornwall. She explains that she is afraid of being poisoned by her dentist husband, Edward. Mrs. Pengelly also tells Poirot that her niece, Miss Freda Stanton lived with them in Polgarwith up until a week previously; and she indicates that a certain Jacob Radnor is a friend of the family.

When Poirot and Hastings come to visit the Pengelly's house, they learn of their client's death. Some months later when Edward Pengelly marries his secretary, Miss Marks, public opinion has it that he got rid of his wife. When the body is exhumed, tests reveal that the women had indeed been poisoned, as she had feared. Edward is arrested on a murder charge, but Poirot is convinced of his innocence.

(194)   1951

The Oglander family, father, mother, son John, and daughter, are playing bridge in the drawing-room of their home in Streatham, when in staggers Mademoiselle St. Clair, crying "Murder!" She explains that she had gone to visit Henry Reedburn, the impressario, at his neighbouring villa, but had found him dead in the library. A friend of Valerie St. Clair's, Prince Paul of Maurania, consults Poirot, hoping that he will be able to clear up the murder mystery.

Poirot realises that Valerie is in fact a member of the Oglander family; and his enquiries reveal that Henry Reedburn had been trying to blackmail her.

Although the Oglanders and Valerie had been somewhat estranged, John Oglander had agreed to help Valerie persuade Reedburn to leave his sister alone. However, when John struck the impressario, the consequences were fatal.

(195)   1951

THE SUBMARINE PLANS

Hercule Poirot receives an urgent call to Sharples, the country house of the Minister of Defence, Lord Alloway. Captain Hastings accompanies Poirot, and at Sharples, they make the acquaintance of Admiral Sir Harry Weardale the First Sea Lord, and Lord Alloway's secretary, Fitzroy. Also staying at Sharples are Lady Weardale, her son Ronald, and a certain Mrs Conrad.

Hercule Poirot, learns that a number of plans, including those for a new submarine, had been set out ready for discussion, by Fitzroy, who left the room for only three minutes, during which time, as Lord Alloway had discovered, the submarine plans were stolen.

As Poirot sees it, there is only one possibility. Lord Alloway must have arranged the theft himself, in order to pass the vital plans to the woman blackmailing him – the secret enemy agent, Mrs Conrad. However, the Minister of Defence had taken the precaution of drawing up fake plans for Mrs. Conrad, while arranging also that she would have no reason to doubt their validity.

(196)   1951

THE ADVENTURE OF THE CLAPHAM COOK

Captain Hastings expresses some surprise when he learns that Poirot is to attempt to solve the case of the missing cook, when consulted by the cook's employer, Mrs. Todd.

Mrs. Todd explains that after her weekly day off, the cook failed to return. Significantly, the Todds also have a paying guest, a Mr. Simpson, who works in the Bank.

Another bank employee, Davis, curiously disappears on the same day as the cook — and is suspected of having stolen £50,000.

(197)   1951

THE ADVENTURE OF THE
CHRISTMAS PUDDING

The son of the ruler of an Eastern State, Prince Ali, is paying a visit to London. While spending an evening with a certain lady, whom we shall call 'X', both a famous royal ruby, and 'X' disappear. Mr. Jesmond, a public servant, convinces Hercule Poirot of the necessity of avoiding a scandal. Knowing that a friend of 'X', a Mr. Desmond Lee-Wortley, is to spend a few days at Christmas at the home of Colonel and Mrs. Lacey as a friend of their grand-daughter, Sarah, Poirot manages to wangle an invitation. There he finds Miss 'X', pretending to be Lee-Wortley's sister.

When Miss 'X' and her 'brother' hear that a detective is a house guest, Miss 'X' hides the stolen royal ruby in the pudding to be eaten on New Year's Day. However, the Christmas pudding has an unfortunate accident – and the second pudding is produced on Christmas Day. Colonel Lacey finds the royal ruby inside the pudding – and Poirot tricks the thieves into leaving the country, with a paste replica.

Remarks: Alternative title is The Theft of the Royal Ruby

(198)   1960

THE MYSTERY OF THE
SPANISH CHEST

Charles Rich, a bachelor, has invited for a party Arnold and Margharita Clayton, Jock McLaren, Jeremy and Linda Spence, Mr. and Mrs. Adam. Before the party Arnold visits Charles' apartment to tell him that he can't come, but his wife will be there. As Charles is not in, Arnold is seen to the sitting-room by the manservant William Burgess to write a note; Burgess goes to the kitchen. When Charles comes in, Arnold has gone, unseen by Burgess.

The next morning Burgess discovers the body of Arnold in an old Spanish chest; stabbed through the neck with a small stiletto. Charles is arrested and Poirot is asked by Margharita to find the murderer, because she is sure that Charles is innocent.

(199)   1960

GREENSHAW'S FOLLY

Many years ago, Nathaniel Greenshaw built a house which came to be known as Greenshaw's Folly, and which is now occupied by Nathaniel's grand-daughter, Miss Katherine Dorothy Greenshaw. One of Katherine's sisters, called Nettie, has an actor son named Nat Fletcher.

When Katherine Greenshaw makes a will leaving everything to her house-keeper, Mrs. Cresswell, she asks Raymond West and his friend Horace Bindler to witness it.

Soon afterwards, Katherine Greenshaw is found dead, murdered by a shot from a bow and arrow.

(200)   1960

DOUBLE SIN

Hercule Poirot and Captain Hastings have a holiday in Ebermonth. Poirot receives a letter from Joseph Aarons in Charlock Bay, in which Joseph asks him to come over for a business-talk.

Poirot and Hastings go to Charlock Bay by motor coach. On this coach they meet Mary Durant, also going to Charlock Bay to sell a collection of miniatures for her aunt, Miss Elizabeth Penn, to an American gentleman, Mr. J. Bakerwood. Miss Penn has an antique shop in Ebermonth; and Mary is learning the business.

In Monkhampton, Norton Kane, mixes his suitcase with Mary's.

In Charlock Bay Mary tells Poirot that the miniatures have been stolen. But Poirot knows better.

(201)   1961

WASP'S NEST

John Harrison and Claude Langton, are old acquaintances of Hercule Poirot. One day Poirot sees John leaving the house of a certain doctor with an expression on his face that can only mean sentence of death.

Poirot goes to visit John, and on the way accidentally sees in the poison book of a chemist that Claude has bought cyanide of potassium. Poirot knows that Miss Molly Dean, who was engaged first to Claude and then to John, is again turning to Claude.

John's plan was: Claude buys cyanide for John, to be used to destroy a wasps' nest, but when Claude brings it John will commit suicide, and Claude will be accused of murder. Poirot prevents the crime.

(202)   1961

THE DRESSMAKER'S DOLL

Alicia Coombe, who owns a dressmaker's shop in London, has received a puppet doll, but she doesn't know from where or from whom.

Several people including Sybil Fox, the shop manageress, Mrs. Fellow-Brown, a customer and Mrs. Grooves, the cleaner, are uneasy about the doll, because it seems to have a life of its own.

One day, when the doll is 'occupying' a room other than that reserved for her, Alicia throws the doll out of the window.

A child in the street takes the doll, because – as the child says – the doll wants to be loved.

(203)   1961

THE DOUBLE CLUE

Mr. Marcus Hardman has invited for a party Mr. Johnston, a South African millionaire, the Countess Vera Rossakoff, a Russian refugée, Mr. Bernard Parker, a friend of Marcus, and Lady Runcorn.

After everyone has gone, Marcus discovers that his safe is open and an emerald necklace with rubies has been stolen.

He doesn't want a scandal and therefore he asks the help of Poirot, who is accompanied by Captain Hastings.

Poirot finds in the safe a glove and a cigarette case with the initials 'P' and 'B': a double clue.

He discovers that the glove is one of Parker's and that the case has been left by the Countess (in Russian a 'B' is an 'V' and a 'P' a 'R').

(204)   1961

While using the stage name of Zobeiden, the dancer, Mary Moss has an affair with a member of an Eastern Royal House, who makes her the gift of some jewels.

Some time later the dancer marries Walter Edward St. John, and gives birth to their daughter, who is named Jewell.

However, after Walter is imprisoned, and Mary Moss dies, Jewell is raised by the Mundy's in Chipping Cleghorn.

When the foster parents are taken ill, Walter St. John escapes from prison, places his late wife's jewels in safe custody and buys a ticket to Chipping Cleghorn.

There Walter is pursued and shot at by two men. He seeks sanctuary in the church, where he is found by the vicar's wife, Blanch, who enlists the aid of her aunt, Miss Marple.

(205)   1961

THE VEILED LADY

A veiled lady consults Poirot and Hastings.

She is Lady Millicent Castle Vaughan, engaged to the Duke of Southshire, and has in the past written an indiscreet letter to a soldier who has since died.

Mr. Lavington now possesses the letter and is blackmailing Lady Millicent.

Poirot and Hastings steal the Chinese Puzzle box, which contains the letter, from Lavington's house.

However, Millicent wants more than the letter. She is also interested in a box of jewels stolen from a shop in Bond Street.

(206)   1924

Theodora Darrell is leaving her husband, Richard Darrell, to go with Vincent Easton to The Transvaal.

In Dover, Theo reads in a newspaper that Richard's firm has collapsed and, out of loyalty she goes back to London. Richard asks her to go to Vincent and ask him for some papers, which are incriminating for Richard.

After she has done this, she learns that Richard supposed that she could get these papers at the cost of her honour; that is enough for Theo to leave Richard for ever.

(207)   1971

Mrs. Joyce Lambert is a widow; her husband Michael died during the war. His last present to Joyce was a terrier: Terry. Joyce is looking for a job, but only a job in which she can keep Terry, and so she is still jobless.

She is so completely desperate, that she promises Arthur Halliday, whom she hates, to marry him on condition that Terry can stay with her.

Then Terry dies.

Joyce takes a job abroad at the house of Mr. Allaby, by coincidence the same man who helped her to take Terry to the veterinarian.

(208)   1971

THE LOST MINE

Poirot tells Hastings of the way in which he received fourteen thousand shares in the Burma Mines Ltd. as a reward.

The present directors had approached Mr. Wu Ling, who possessed a record of the mine, and asked him to travel to London, but he didn't show up at the meeting with the directors.

Later it was stated that he drowned in the Thames.

Mr. Pearson, one of the directors, asked Poirot to work together with Inspector Miller; Miller was interested in the murder, Poirot had to be interested primarily in the papers relating to the mine.

(209)   1924

Hastings tells a story, in which Poirot tells how he once made a fool of himself.

A M. Paul Déroulard had married a rich lady in Brussels. Two years later she died, leaving her estate to Paul.

The inheritance for Paul included the house at Avenue Louise, the inmates of which were — apart from the servants — Paul, the mother of Paul: Madame la Baronne and Virginie Mesnard, a cousin of the late Madame Déroulard.

Paul had died one evening in the presence of two guests, M. de Saint Alard and Mr. John Wilson. Although the cause was said to be heart failure, Virginie asked Poirot to investigate. Poirot's attention was attracted by a pink chocolate box with a blue lid and the fact that Paul was fond of chocolate and that the box was still full.

A servant brought the old box, which was blue with a pink lid. It appears that Madame, who had bad eyesight, had opened the full box by mistake and changed the lids.

(210)   1924

WHODUNNITS
AND
INDEXES

WHODUNNITS
NOVELS

1 Alfred Inglethorp, with Evelyn Howard as his accomplice.
2 Mr. Brown.
3 Marthe Daubreuil.
4 Harry Rayburn killed L.B. Carton; Sir Eustace Pedler killed Madame Nadina.
5 Mademoiselle Brun, with King Victor as her accomplice.
6 Dr. James Sheppard.
7 'The Big Four'.
8 Derek Kettering, with Ada Mason (Kitty Kidd) as his associate.)
9 Jimmy Thesiger, with Loraine Wade as his accomplice.
10 Mrs. Protheroe, with Lawrence Redding as her accomplice.
11 Major Burnaby.
12 Nick Buckley.
13 Jane Wilkinson (Lady Edgware).
14 Moira Nicholson and Roger Bassington-ffrench.
15 –
16 Franklin Clarke.
17 Norman Gale, with Anne Morisot as his accomplice.
18 Sir Charles Cartwright.
19 Anne Meredith.
20 Frederick Bosner (Dr. Leidner).
21 Jacqueline de Bellefort with Simon Doyle as her accomplice.
22 Bella Tanios.
23 Lady Westholme.
24 Superintendent Sugden.
25 Miss Honoria Waynflete.
26 Judge Lawrence Wargrave.
27 Mary Riley (Nurse Hopkins).
28 Mr. Alistair Blunt and his wife Gerda Grant.
29 –
30 Edward Corrington (Patrick Redfern) with Christine Deverill (Christine Redfern) as his accomplice.
31 Mark Gaskell and his wife Josephine Turner.
32 Elsa Greer.
33 Mr. Symmington.
34 Nevile Strange.
35 Victor Drake and Ruth Lessing.
36 Yahmose.

WHODUNNITS
NOVELS

37 Gerda Christow.
38 Rowley Cloade killed Charles Trenton; Major Porter shot himself; David Hunter murdered Rosaleen Cloade.
39 Josephine Leonides.
40 Letitia (Charlotte) Blacklock.
41 –
42 Lewis Serrocold.
43 Robin Upward (Evelyn Hope).
44 Miss Gilchrist.
45 Lancelot Fortescue killed Rex Fortescue (using Gladys Martin), Gladys Martin and Adèle Aristides.
46 Monsieur Aristides.
47 Nigel Stanley (Nigel Chapman) and Valerie Hobhouse.
48 Sir George Stubbs and Hattie Stubbs: James Folliat and his wife.
49 Dr. Quimper
50 Kirstin Landstrom, pushed by Jack Argyle.
51 Ann Shapland killed Miss Springer and Miss Blanche; Miss Chadwick killed Miss Vansittart.
52 Zachariah Osborne.
53 Marina Gregg.
54 Miss Martindale; Mr. and Mrs. Bland.
55 Tim Kendal.
56 Lady Bess Sedgwick is responsible for the robberies; Elvira Blake is the murderess.
57 Frances Cary and Robert Orwell.
58 Michael Rogers and Greta Andersen.
59 Mrs. Lancaster.
60 Mrs. Rowena Drake and Michael Garfield.
61 Sir James Kleek and Mrs. Cortman.
62 Clotilde Bradbury-Scott.
63 Dolly pushed Molly over the cliff; Alistair killed Dolly and himself.
64 Miss Iris Mullins (Dodo).
65 Stephen Norton.
66 James Kennedy.

WHODUNNITS
SHORT STORIES

67 Gregory Rolf.
68 Mr Maltravers was murdered by his wife.
69 Miss Elsa Hardt.
70 Roger Havering and his wife.
71 Mr. Shaw.
72 Dr. Robert Ames.
73 The hotel chambermaid and the valet.
74 Captain Daniels.
75 Mr. Davenheim.
76 Graves.
77 Poirot discovers a second will.
78 —
79 Jeanette Smith.
80 The pearl was stolen by Elise.
81 Dymchurch.
82 The murderer was Sir Arthur Merivale.
83 —
84 —
85 Gilda Glen's husband is the murderer.
86 Ryder is the counterfeiters leader.
87 Mr. Hollaby assisted by his son.
88 The killer is Miss Logan.
89 Una Drake has an identical twin sister — Vera.
90 The young gentleman and Dr. O'Neill are the same person.
91 —
92 The Russian is Mrs. Cortland Van Snyder.
93 Eleanor is now married to Alex Portal.
94 The murderer is Richard Scott.
95 Hartwell and the gardener John Mathias are the same person.
96 The murderer is Lord George Barnaby.
97 The Countess was once the croupier's wife.
98 Anthony Cosden is the father of the woman's son.
99 The maid drowned and Beatrice lost her memory.
100 Philip plans Gillian's death. Satterthwaite saves her.
101 Hugo Charnley.
102 David Keeley.
103 —
104 Anna Denman is the same person as the Russian dancer.
105 Mr. Jones planned the murder of his wife.
106 Richard was killed by Elliot.
107 Newman was responsible for the robbery.
108 Denis murdered Margery.

109 Emma gave Simon Clode a fountain pen filled with disappearing ink when he was writing his new will.

110 Geoffrey was murdered by his father.

111 Mary was murdered by her nurse.

112 Amy drowned Mary.

113 The murderess is Greta.

114 Jack murdered Gladys and swapped the bodies.

115 Ambrose Beray murdered his ward, Sylvia.

116 Cohen is Sir Joseph Salmon.

117 Mrs. Bartlett killed Rose.

118 Dr. Rose in attempting to murder his wife killed himself and the nun.

119 Jack Trent is mad and he killed Alington.

120 —

121 —

122 —

123 Charles Ridgeway provided Patrick's voice in the hope of obtaining his aunt's money.

124 Romaine and Mrs. Mogson are the same person.

125 The mysterious cries for help were perpetrated by Felicie and Larington.

126 Lady Carmichael caused Arthur's lunacy.

127 —

128 —

129 The Clevelands made their own daughter Magdale act as the adopted child.

130 —

131 Gerald dies from shock after his wife tells him she had poisoned her previous husbands.

132 —

133 Mr. Crabtree took the money.

134 —

135 —

136 The Duchess.

137 —

138 The two policemen are bogus and are part of the Patterson gang.

139 Mary devised everything to test George.

140 Detective Inspector Merrilees is arrested.

141 Paula Nazorkoff murders Bréon in revenge.

142 —

143 —

144 Mr. Pyne discovers that the so-called 'stolen' ring is in fact a paste replica.

145 —

146 –
147 –
148 Edward has been the victim of blackmail.
149 The murderer is Mr. Samuel Long.
150 Lady Esther Carr died in the fall.
151 When accused of stealing Miss Blundell's earring, Dr. Carver confesses.
152 West reveals that he was Lady Ariadne's lover.
153 Mrs. Peter's son is returned and the jewel thieves sent off to prison.
154 Jane has made Barbara's suicide look like murder.
155 Lord Mayfield has stolen the plans in order to exchange them with Mrs. Vanderlyn for old incriminating letters.
156 Lin Garol.
157 Tony and Marjorie planned the murder.
158 Eve/Maria was responsible for replacing the Morning Star with a replica.
159 Major Curtiss drugged Edward with a drink laced with a narcotic, and then killed him.
160 Mary and her husband poisoned the oysters.
161 –
162 Barton made an attempt on Pauline's life.
163 Mrs. Curruthers, one of the women guests.
164 The victim was shot by Cornworthy.
165 –
166 Colonel Clapperton killed his wife.
167 –
168 Nurse Harrison started the unfortunate rumours.
169 –
170 Enquiries reveal Marrascaud to be the killer.
171 –
172 Mrs. Rice and her daughter are blackmailers.
173 Hugh Chandler is not mad, but is being poisoned by Admiral Chandler.
174 General Grant has used each of his daughters as a drugs distributor.
175 The whole episode was designed as a means of smuggling the Rubens out of England.
176 Dr. Andersen.
177 Patrick Casey's daughter became a nun and Emery Power agrees to return the goblet into the keeping of the nuns.
178 The club is owned by Dr. Cunningham and is at the centre of a drugs operation.

179 Hubert Lytcham Roche has been a victim of his secretary, Geoffrey Keene.
180 Detective Sergeant Trotter.
181 –
182 Miss Politt.
183 Lavinia and Emily Skinner.
184 Harry Laxton paid the caretaker's wife to scare Louise.
185 The murderer is Miss Garnett's friend, Donovan.
186 Waverly enlisting the help of the butler Tredwell.
187 Dr. George Ramsey.
188 Paul is the murderer, and Laura his accomplice.
189 Owen Trefusis was the murderer.
190 Red Nanky and his accomplice, Jane Mason.
191 Davidson was responsible for Lord Cronshaw's death.
192 –
193 Hugo Lemesurier murdered his brothers Vincent and John.
194 Jacob Radnor admits to having wanted to marry the niece, Freda, in order to get his hands on the money.
195 Hercule Poirot, observing that the King of Clubs was missing, knew that the story had been a fabrication.
196 Lord Alloway stole the plans as he was being blackmailed.
197 Poirot reveals the thief to be Simpson.
198 –
199 Arnold was stabbed by Jock McLaren.
200 Miss Marple reveals Mrs. Cresswell and her son to be the killers.
201 The miniatures were sold by Miss Penn who then reported the theft.
202 –
203 –
204 –
205 –
206 Gertie, who played the role of Lady Millicent.
207 –
208 –
209 Mr. Pearson.
210 M. de Saint Alard is the murderer.

NUMERICAL REFERENCE

1	1920	The Mysterious Affair at Styles
2	1922	The Secret Adversary
3	1923	The Murder on the Links
4	1924	The Man in the Brown Suit
5	1925	The Secret of Chimneys
6	1926	The Murder of Roger Ackroyd
7	1927	The Big Four
8	1928	The Mystery of the Blue Train
9	1929	The Seven Dials Mystery
10	1930	The Murder at the Vicarage
11	1931	The Sittaford Mystery or Murder at Hazelmoor
12	1932	Peril at End House
13	1933	Lord Edgware Dies or Thirteen at Dinner
14	1934	Why Didn't They Ask Evans? or The Boomerang Clue
15	1934	Murder on the Orient Express or Murder in the Calais Coach
16	1935	The ABC Murders
17	1935	Death in the Clouds or Death in the Air
18	1935	Three Act Tragedy or Murder in Three Acts
19	1936	Cards on the Table
20	1936	Murder in Mesopotamia
21	1937	Death on the Nile
22	1937	Dumb Witness or Poirot Loses a Client
23	1938	Appointment with Death
24	1938	Hercule Poirot's Christmas or Murder for Christmas
25	1939	Murder Is Easy or Easy to Kill
26	1939	Ten Little Niggers or And Then There Were None or Ten Little Indians
27	1940	Sad Cypress
28	1940	One, Two, Buckle My Shoe or The Patriotic Murders
29	1941	N or M?
30	1941	Evil under the Sun
31	1942	The Body in the Library
32	1943	Five Little Pigs or Murder in Retrospect
33	1943	The Moving Finger
34	1944	Towards Zero or Come and Be Hanged
35	1945	Sparkling Cyanide or Remembered Death
36	1945	Death Comes As the End
37	1946	The Hollow or Murder After Hours
38	1948	Taken at the Flood or There Is a Tide
39	1949	Crooked House
40	1950	A Murder Is Announced
41	1951	They Came to Baghdad
42	1952	They Do It With Mirrors or Murder With Mirrors
43	1952	Mrs. McGinty's Dead or Blood Will Tell

44	1953	After the Funeral or Funerals Are Fatal
45	1953	A Pocket Full of Rye
46	1954	Destination Unknown or So Many Steps to Death
47	1955	Hickory, Dickory, Dock or Hickory, Dickory, Death
48	1956	Dead Man's Folly
49	1957	4:50 From Paddington or What Mrs. McGillicuddy Saw
50	1958	Ordeal By Innocence
51	1959	Cat Among the Pigeons
52	1961	The Pale Horse
53	1962	The Mirror Crack'd From Side to Side
54	1963	The Clocks
55	1964	A Caribbean Mystery
56	1965	At Bertram's Hotel
57	1966	Third Girl
58	1967	Endless Night
59	1968	By the Pricking of my Thumbs
60	1969	Hallowe'en Party
61	1970	Passenger to Frankfurt
62	1971	Nemesis
63	1972	Elephants Can Remember
64	1973	Postern of Fate
65	1975	Curtain: Poirot's Last Case
66	1976	Sleeping Murder (Miss Marple's Last Case)
67	1924	The Adventure of 'The Western Star'
68	1924	The Tragedy at Marsdon Manor
69	1924	The Adventure of the Cheap Flat
70	1924	The Mystery of Hunter's Lodge
71	1924	The Million Dollar Bond Robbery
72	1924	The Adventure of the Egyptian Tomb
73	1924	The Jewel Robbery at the 'Grand Metropolitan'
74	1924	The Kidnapped Prime Minister
75	1924	The Disappearance of Mr. Davenheim
76	1924	The Adventure of the Italian Nobleman
77	1924	The Case of the Missing Will
78	1929	A Fairy in the Flat
79	1929	A Pot of Tea
80	1929	The Affair of the Pink Pearl
81	1929	The Adventure of the Sinister Stranger
82	1929	Finessing the King and the Gentleman Dressed in Newspaper
83	1929	The Case of the Missing Lady
84	1929	Blindman's Buff
85	1929	The Man in the Mist
86	1929	The Crackler
87	1929	The Sunningdale Mystery
88	1929	The House of Lurking Death
89	1929	The Unbreakable Alibi
90	1929	The Clergyman's Daughter and the Red House
91	1929	The Ambassador's Boots
92	1929	The Man Who Was No. 16
93	1930	The Coming of Mr. Quin
94	1930	The Shadow on the Glass
95	1930	At the 'Bells and Motley'
96	1930	The Sign in the Sky
97	1930	The Soul of the Croupier
98	1930	The Man From the Sea
99	1930	The Voice in the Dark
100	1930	The Face of Helen

101	1930	The Dead Harlequin
102	1930	The Bird With the Broken Wing
103	1930	The World's End
104	1930	Harlequin's Lane
105	1932	The Tuesday Night Club
106	1932	The Idol House of Astarte
107	1932	Ingots of Gold
108	1932	The Bloodstained Pavement
109	1932	Motive vs. Opportunity
110	1932	The Thumb Mark of St. Peter
111	1932	The Blue Geranium
112	1932	The Companion
113	1932	The Four Suspects
114	1932	A Christmas Tragedy
115	1932	The Herb of Death
116	1932	The Affair at the Bungalow
117	1932	Death by Drowning
118	1933	The Hound of Death
119	1933	The Red Signal
120	1933	The Fourth Man
121	1933	The Gipsy
122	1933	The Lamp
123	1933	Wireless or Where There's a Will
124	1933	The Witness for the Prosecution
125	1933	The Mystery of the Blue Jar
126	1933	The Strange Case of Sir Arthur Carmichael
127	1933	The Call of Wings
128	1933	The Last Seance
129	1933	SOS
130	1934	The Listerdale Mystery
131	1934	Philomel Cottage
132	1934	The Girl in the Train
133	1934	Sing a Song of Sixpence
134	1934	The Manhood of Edward Robinson
135	1934	Accident
136	1934	Jane in Search of a Job
137	1934	A Fruitful Sunday
138	1934	Mr. Eastwood's Adventure or The Mystery of the Spanish Shawl
139	1934	The Golden Ball
140	1934	The Rajah's Emerald
141	1934	Swan Song
142	1934	The Case of the Middle-Aged Wife
143	1934	The Case of the Discontented Soldier
144	1934	The Case of the Distressed Lady
145	1934	The Case of the Discontented Husband
146	1934	The Case of the City Clerk
147	1934	The Case of the Rich Woman
148	1934	Have You Got Everything You Want?
149	1934	The Gate of Baghdad
150	1934	The House at Shiraz
151	1934	The Pearl of Price
152	1934	Death on the Nile
153	1934	The Oracle at Delphi
154	1937	Murder in the Mews
155	1937	The Incredible Theft
156	1937	Dead Man's Mirror
157	1937	Triangle at Rhodes
158	1939	The Regatta Mystery
159	1939	The Mystery of the Baghdad Chest
160	1939	How Does Your Garden Grow?
161	1939	Problem at Pollensa Bay

162	1939	Yellow Iris
163	1939	Miss Marple Tells a Story
164	1939	The Dream
165	1939	In a Glass Darkly
166	1939	Problem at Sea or
		Murder at Sea
167	1947	The Nemean Lion
168	1947	The Lernean Hydra
169	1947	The Arcadian Deer
170	1947	The Erymanthian Boar
171	1947	The Augean Stables
172	1947	The Stymphalean Birds
173	1947	The Cretan Bull
174	1947	The Horses of Diomedes
175	1947	The Girdle of Hyppolita
176	1947	The Flock of Geryon
177	1947	The Apples of the Hesperides
178	1947	The Capture of Cerberus
179	1948	The Second Gong
180	1950	Three Blind Mice
181	1950	Strange Jest
182	1950	Tape-Measure Murder
183	1950	The Case of the Perfect Maid
184	1950	The Case of the Caretaker
185	1950	The Third-Floor Flat
186	1950	The Adventure of Johnnie Waverly
187	1950	Four and Twenty Blackbirds
188	1950	The Love Detectives
189	1951	The Under Dog
190	1951	The Plymouth Express
191	1951	The Affair at the Victory Ball
192	1951	The Market Basing Mystery
193	1951	The Lemesurier Inheritance
194	1951	The Cornish Mystery
195	1951	The King of Clubs
196	1951	The Submarine Plans
197	1951	The Adventure of the Clapham Cook
198	1960	The Adventure of the Christmas Pudding or
		The Theft of the Royal Baby
199	1960	The Mystery of the Spanish Chest
200	1960	Greenshaw's Folly
201	1961	Double Sin
202	1961	Wasps' Nest
203	1961	The Dressmaker's Doll
204	1961	The Double Clue
205	1961	Sanctuary
206	1924	The Veiled Lady
207	1971	Magnolia Blossom
208	1971	Next to a Dog
209	1924	The Lost Mine
210	1924	The Chocolate Box

ALPHABETICAL REFERENCE

ALPHABETICAL REFERENCE

ALPHABETICAL REFERENCE

SHORT STORY
COLLECTIONS

collection	1	1924	Poirot Investigates
collection	2	1929	Partners in Crime
collection	3	1930	The Mysterious Mr. Quin or
			The Passing of Mr. Quin
collection	4	1932	The Thirteen Problems or
			The Tuesday Club Murders
collection	5	1933	The Hound of Death
collection	6	1934	The Listerdale Mystery
collection	7	1934	Parker Pyne Investigates or
			Mr. Parker Pyne, Detective
collection	8	1937	Murder in the Mews or
			Dead Man's Mirror
collection	9	1939	The Regatta Mystery
collection	10	1947	The Labours of Hercules
collection	11	1948	The Witness for the Prosecution
collection	12	1950	Three Blind Mice and Other Stories or
		·	The Mousetrap and Other Stories
collection	13	1951	The Under Dog
collection	14	1960	The Adventure of the Christmas Pudding
collection	15	1961	Double Sin
collection	16	1961	13 For Luck
collection	17	1965	Surprise Surprise
collection	18	1966	13 Clues for Miss Marple
collection	19	1971	The Golden Ball
collection	20	1974	Poirot's Early Cases
collection	21	1979	Miss Marple's Final Cases

collection 1 contains: 67, 68, 69, 70, 71 72 73, 74, 75, 76, 77
(in first edition also 206, 209, 210)

collection 2 contains: 78, 79, 80, 81, 82, 83, 84, 85, 86, 87, 88, 89,
90, 91, 92

collection 3 contains: 93, 94, 95, 96, 97, 98, 99, 100, 101, 102, 103,
104

collection 4 contains: 105, 106, 107, 108, 109, 110, 111, 112, 113,
114, 115, 116, 117

collection 5 contains: 118, 119, 120, 121, 122, 123, 124, 125, 126,
127, 128, 129

collection 6 contains: 130, 131, 132, 133, 134, 135, 136, 137, 138,
139, 140, 141

collection 7 contains: 142, 143, 144, 145, 146, 147, 148, 149, 150,
151, 152, 153

collection 8 contains: 154, 155, 156, 157

collection 9 contains: 158, 159, 160, 161, 162, 163, 164, 165, 166

collection 10 contains: 167, 168, 169, 170, 171, 172, 173, 174, 175,
176, 177, 178

collection 11 contains: 124, 119, 120, 129, 123, 125, 133, 138, 131,
135, 179

collection 12 contains: 180, 181, 182, 183, 184, 185, 186, 187, 188

collection 13 contains: 189, 190, 191, 192, 193, 194, 195, 196, 197

collection 14 contains: 198, 199, 189, 187, 164, 200

collection 15 contains: 201, 202, 198, 203, 200, 204, 128, 205

collection 16 contains: 206, 167, 175, 192, 182, 111, 113, 100, 102,
158, 161, 89, 135

collection 17 contains: 201, 169, 186, 123, 200, 183, 95, 144, 185,
190

collection 18 contains: 111, 184, 183, 112, 113, 200, 115, 109, 205,
181, 182, 110, 108

collection 19 contains: 130, 132, 134, 136, 137, 139, 140, 141, 118,
121, 122, 126, 127, 207, 208

collection 20 contains: 191, 197, 186, 204, 195, 193, 209, 190, 210,
196, 185, 201, 192, 202, 206, 166, 160

collection 21 contains: 205, 181, 182, 184, 183, 163, 203, 165

MAIN CHARACTER REFERENCES

Miss Jane Marple

10	31	33	44	42	49	53
55	56	62	66	105	106	107
108	109	110	111	112	113	114
115	116	117	163	181	182	183
184	200	205				

Hercule Poirot

1	3	7	8	12	13	15
16	17	18	19	20	21	22
23	24	27	28	30	32	37
38	43	44	45	47	48	51
54	57	60	63	65	67	68
69	70	71	72	73	74	75
76	77	154	155	156	157	158
160	162	164	166	167	168	169
170	171	172	173	174	175	176
177	178	179	185	186	187	189
190	191	192	193	194	195	196
197	198	199	201	202	204	206
209	210					

Tommy and Tuppence

2	29	59	64	78	79	80
81	82	83	84	85	86	87
88	89	90	91	92		

Parker Pyne

142	143	144	145	146	147	148
149	150	151	152	153	158	161

Colonel Race

4	35

Superintendent Battle

5	9	34

255